PENGUIN BOOKS

THE FORCE BEHIND THE FORCES

Swapnil Pandey is a popular author with a wide audience base. She loves to compile stories about life in the Indian Army and has previously authored *Soldier's Girl* (2017) and *Love Story of a Commando* (2019). Swapnil married into the *fauji* tribe thirteen years ago; since then her nomadic life in Army cantonments all over the country amongst extraordinary men and women has inspired her to come up with the most extraordinary stories.

Being a true believer in the nation's responsibility towards the well-being of its soldiers and their families, she attempts to provide an authentic glimpse of the much-coveted Army life and its struggles in her work.

Also a professional blogger, Swapnil is a societal influencer whose voice has made an impact in highlighting the struggles and issues faced by military families.

Swapnil is an alumnus of Birla Institute of Technology, Mesra, and has worked with organizations such as Wipro and HDFC. She has also taught at Lovely Professional University and the Army Public School, to name a few of her ever-changing job profiles as the wife of an army officer. She has finally settled in the role of a full-time author.

You can read her blogs on girlandworld.com. She can be contacted at teamgirlandworld@gmail.com. You can also be part of her social media family on these platforms:

Twitter: @swapy6
Facebook: Author Swapnil Pandey
Instagram: swapnil_pandey_author

THE FORCE BEHIND THE FORCES

Stories of Brave Indian Army Wives

SWAPNIL PANDEY

PENGUIN BOOKS

An imprint of Penguin Random House

PENGUIN BOOKS

USA | Canada | UK | Ireland | Australia
New Zealand | India | South Africa | China

Penguin Books is part of the Penguin Random House group of companies
whose addresses can be found at global.penguinrandomhouse.com

Published by Penguin Random House India Pvt. Ltd
4th Floor, Capital Tower 1, MG Road,
Gurugram 122 002, Haryana, India

| Penguin
Random House
India

First published in Penguin Books by Penguin Random House India 2021

This book is a work of non-fiction. The views and opinions expressed in the book
are those of the author only and do not reflect or represent the views and opinions
held by any other person.

This book is based on a variety of sources including interviews and interactions
conducted by the author with the persons mentioned in the manuscript. It reflects
the author's own understanding and conception of such materials and/or can be
verified by research.

The objective of this book is not to hurt any sentiments or be biased in favour
of or against any particular person, region, caste, society, gender, creed, nation
or religion.

ISBN 9780143453529

Typeset in Adobe Caslon Pro by Manipal Technologies Limited, Manipal
Printed at Thomson Press India Ltd, New Delhi

www.penguin.co.in

When we are apart, you still have my heart,
The nation feels safe under your guard.
You have your orders from your Command,
To go fight a war,
To be sent away is always a plan.

My faith tells me nothing will fall apart,
And my tears are only a matter of chance.
I am proud of what you do,
and the person you are.
But, my love,
it's tough to be a soldier, and
even tougher to be his better half.

Dedicated to all the veer naris who, in their quest of finding strength, inspire us all. Know you are not alone and the nation stands with you all.

Contents

Foreword

The author, Swapnil Pandey, who has written many books on defence lives, and who herself is an Army wife, depicts pain and pride, valour and victory, and love and care in the Army, with great sensitivity in this book titled *The Force Behind the Forces*. She has covered the lives of seven veer naris and their families. Each has some similarity with the others, and yet plenty of uniqueness in its portrayal of dealing with personal loss, running of the household, planning for the future, bringing up the children, and helping the wives face the realities of life. The *veer nari* herself needs to understand how her young offsprings would deal with the future they do not even comprehend. She is expected to be strong, caring and compassionate for the young as much as for the rest. The burden of expectations is not easy to bear.

Swapnil has managed to extract the 'real self' of the veer nari, with patience and sanctity. I am confident she will continue to bring the bravery and strength of such women to her readers, in the future as well. This will help the nation to know the sacrifices of a brave woman who not only stands with her soldier in the times of peace and war, but also continues to march on if he unfortunately does not return home.

Having worked in the War Widows Association, New Delhi, for over a decade, first as Secretary and now as President, I have come across many cases where war/conflict widows have been through all kinds of difficulties yet they choose to live with great pride in the sacrifice their husbands have made. I feel a lot more should be done by the nation. My best wishes for the response this book deserves, and the empathy the reading should generate. I wish to add that I have felt each and every emotion the brave naris have been through, and would have to live with forever. May God give them strength and the ability to live a dignified life despite their biggest loss.

Damayanti V Tambay
Wife of Flt Lt Vijay Vasant Tambay
Missing-in-action
1971 Indo-Pak war
Arjuna Awardee (Badminton) &
President,
War Widows Association, New Delhi

A Note to Readers by
Dr V. Mohini Giri, Padma Bhushan

I was eight years old when I first saw my mother as a widow. I saw her struggle, looking after all the children, providing for the family and also dealing with life in general. She was not single, but a widow, and our society isn't inclusive of widows even today, let alone in those days. This first-hand experience of a widow's plight left a deep impact on my mind. Then came the 1971 War. Bombs exploded, troops were deployed, aircrafts buzzed in the sky, and many women and children were displaced. Mr Melville De Mellow (Padma Shri)—the Indian radio broadcaster with All India Radio—kept us hooked with his presentations on war. When the minute-to-minute updates, even from far-flung areas, reached us in the Rashtrapati Bhavan, there was a sense of victory, but also an acknowledgement of the grief of losing comrades and the dilemma of dealing with the new challenges that lay ahead. My father-in-law, the fourth President of India Shri Varahagiri Venkata Giri, felt deeply for our soldiers and their families. He considered it his utmost duty to serve those who had served the nation, even at the cost of their lives. There would be interactions with many high-profile dignitaries; Chief of the Army Staff Sam Manekshaw, ADCs, Prime Minister Indira Gandhi, ministers, social activists, scholars and more who kept visiting to meet the President, discussing various issues, challenges and possible preparations in case of emergency. There was turmoil in the country and anything could have happened. Being the first family of the nation, it was an obligation for us to prepare for the worst.

It was then that my father-in-law asked me to visit railway stations to provide food to the soldiers. It was the least that I could do for them. My mother-in-law also asked me to visit hospitals to look after the well-being of the soldiers being treated there. The hospital visits turned out to be heart-wrenching; one could see the many gruesome costs of our victory; there were dead and wounded in large numbers. Some had their families beside them while some still searched for them. There was hopelessness and chaos.

Those who died in my arms all said to me, 'Please look after my family!'

The war had ended, but there were so many widows who were distressed, clueless and rendered destitute. Emotionally derailed, the widows and families needed support that could uplift them and take their lives forward. Then, the final push came in the form of Ms Rupa Mehta.

After the war, in the honour of the first President and the eventual Prime Minister of Bangladesh Sheikh Mujibur Rahman, a banquet was held at the Asoka Hotel, New Delhi. It was also an occasion to celebrate the historic victory of the Indian Armed Forces. The forces had arrived on the world scene announcing complete dominance. Ms Rupa Mehta, who was employed at the hotel in the housekeeping department, knew about me and the social service I had been doing for the soldiers and their families. She was a widow of the 1962 Chinese aggression and she talked to me about her late husband. Her struggles in search of her soldier had been immense. She had visited China three times, searched every nook and corner possible, had even looked among the beggars, at the bearers, and anybody she came across, to see if her husband was alive. It was a traumatizing experience for her.

The turmoil inside me was now difficult to contain. Observing a series of events involving people in agony, suffering and anguish combined with the plight of several distressed war widows, I was now determined to make special efforts towards the cause. I called all the war widows from 1962, 1965 and the 1971 wars to the Rashtrapati Bhavan for a meeting. After that historic meeting, we decided to take up their cause and registered an organization called the War Widows Association in January 1972. The forum was started with an indomitable spirit to stand up for war widows and to let them know that they were not alone and that the nation stood beside them. We started the organization with literally just one rupee, which later grew into a large project in the multi-crore building 'Shaheed Bhawan'—established for the rehabilitation of the widows of our soldiers. The war widows now had a place they could call their own. We chose the inverted gun and the left-out helmet in the battleground as our emblem in the memory of soldiers who had left before their time. There was still not much money to go around, but the desire to uplift the lives of the families of our veer soldiers kept us going.

After the war, there was chaos in the whole country; so one could only imagine the young war widows and their trauma. They did not know how to go about getting their pensions, securing their children's education, etc. There were government grants, but most of the young and vulnerable widows living in far-flung areas all across the country did not know how, nor had the will to start their lives again. Here, the War Widows Association helped. We at the Association not only met the emotional needs of the widows at that time, but also worked hard to help them in their rehabilitation by way of procuring gas agencies, vocations, hospital services, government aid, etc. to allow them a smoother transition from a marginalized state to self-sufficiency. In many cases, we were able to support the complete education of children whose fathers had made the supreme sacrifice for their nation. We were also able to resolve the issues of residence through allotment of plots and sanctioning of loans to the widows to build homes where they could lead their lives with dignity. We helped them achieve employment and rehabilitation at many levels.

We had no money to run the day-to-day operations and so we sought the help of many prominent personalities of that time and they generously helped the cause. Rishi Kapoor, who did many fundraising programmes at Shaheed Bhawan, Mehandi Hasan, Hema Malini, Mukesh, Gulam Ali and many more came forward and helped us raise funds, and eventually we were also able to open a training-cum-production unit for the benefit of the women whose soldiers had left them so untimely. I travelled to various states of India and met politicians, ministers and government officials in my quest of supporting war widows even in the rural areas. Many of the chief ministers treated women from the War Widows Association as state guests and supported our cause generously, but some did not bother. However, it would take more than just that to break our belief in our cause. Eventually, we were able to expand the reach of the War Widows Association all across India. We opened training-cum-production centres across many states; built many hostels for the children of soldiers killed in action; and provided skill training to thousands of grieving women who found new goals and purpose in life. After the Kargil War, we also took the initiative to visit Kashmir to hold meetings and make provisions, crossing many hurdles to ensure that our Veer Naris got all the services they required after the war.

This quest of empowering widows of KIA soldiers is still ongoing. There are no wars now, but the tough lives of our soldiers' widows are still a harsh reality. For many vulnerable women whose husbands make the supreme sacrifice in counter-insurgency operations, the grief is still the same, the plight of being left behind is still the same.

It is important for the younger generations today to understand the predicament of the widow of a soldier who is killed to safeguard the collective dreams of the nation. We need more young people to come forward and support this cause. Writers, scholars, media personalities and politicians should all bear their responsibilities towards the families of our bravehearts. These young women face thousands of struggles in their widowhood; not merely monetary, but also emotional. The grave concerns they face include finding a place to stay and their kids' upbringing and schooling, and they often face all this with no means of income at hand. The government and its institutions have limited resources and widows in their day-to-day lives already juggle the dual burdens of social stigma and emotional distress. It is hence imperative that society step up to this cause. So, when I came across Swapnil Pandey, who met me in her journey to draw attention towards the widows of soldiers in the form of her inspirational book *The Force behind the Forces*, I was delighted.

Being an army wife herself, Swapnil illustrates the inimitable courage, sorrow and hardships faced by army wives in a unique style, touching the very core of human emotion. Her non-fictional narrative is an inspiring series of events depicting the massive courage required to make sacrifices for a higher cause. Her diction is pure. Her emotional tales instil moral values while preserving the defence culture at the same time. My heart goes out to all the unforgettable war widows whom I consider victorious.

I wish Swapnil all the best and I also appeal to the countrymen to support her pure endeavour and develop their own sense of duty towards Veer Naris. I would like to end my note to the people of India by saying that we, as a society, need to shed any and all stigmas that result in the exploitative shunning of widows, and instead learn from and imbibe their attitude. Give the wife of the soldier the support and dignity that she so thoroughly deserves. Don't forget that she exists. It is our utmost duty to never forget these women who are usually left to lead a life of oblivion. Thank you, Swapnil, for doing what you are doing. I hope more people follow in your footsteps.

The Force behind the Forces is an equal hero!

Dr V. Mohini Giri (Padma Bhushan)
Founder-Chairperson, War Widows Association
Chairperson of the Guild of Service
Former Chairperson of the
National Commission for Women (1995–1998)

Author's Note

How often do we talk about the women behind the Armed Forces? Maybe when a soldier makes the supreme sacrifice and his woman, much shaken in grief, captures the imagination of the nation for a brief time. For most people, the military wife is a myth, a woman who lives in the shadow of her soldier throughout her life, not that she is not proud of it. However, this book is a humble attempt to tell people that the women behind the forces are actually their driving force.

Writing this book was a brave decision for me. It is not easy to write about broken dreams, lost hopes, and shattered families. I also offer heartfelt gratitude to the women, who chose to share the most painful details of their lives. After all, my questions hovered around the most significant loss in their lives. Indeed, it was courageous of these sheroes to talk about it. There were times when I could not sleep, and there were times when I cried for several consecutive nights, while writing this book.

To listen to their heart-wrenching stories with an unaffected face was the bravest thing I have ever done.

There were many times I almost gave up, but I rose to begin again each time because I believed that these stories should reach the people and tell them that the Armed Forces wives are heroes in equal measure. These stories also illustrate how these women are made of a different mettle, and how their contribution to national freedom is unparalleled. These stories will also push you to bow before the courage and strength of Indian women.

I remember how Karuna, wife of late Lieutenant Commander D.S. Chauhan, who sacrificed his life onboard INS Vikramaditya in 2019, once told me she was desperately searching on Google how veer naris cope with the grief of losing their husbands in the line of duty, and she did not find any answers.

I hope this book will help hundreds of women, just like the women featured in the book, to cope with their grief and let them know they are not alone. I also hope this book will provide courage to all people, who feel broken, to start over again. It is also an attempt to dispel the widely spread myth among the millennials today that all hope is lost and true love does not exist.

If soldiers live a life less ordinary, these are the extraordinary women behind them. Each of them hides a story that will not only touch your heart, but also shake you with its portrayal of immense courage, valour, patience, sacrifice, and the choices of these military wives from time to time. The contrast in their stories will widen your eyes in disbelief.

It is perhaps the easiest task on the planet to fall for that one man in uniform, not a part of the crowd. But it is also extremely tough to lead a different life, and strike a balance with the same uniformed man—who will sometimes behave like a luminary.

Most of the life of a military wife is spent trying to maintain a 'normal' routine. There is a high probability of facing challenges unusual to an average Indian woman. She takes the back seat in everything. You might find an IIT degree, a certificate of 'Employee of the Month' from a major multi-national company, an onsite job offer letter promising several thousand dollars, thrown carelessly in one of her black-painted military trunks. She selflessly puts herself second, sometimes effacing her identity completely. She takes it as her duty towards her soldier, and also towards her nation, to support him since he is directly involved with its security and safety. It is not because she considers herself a lesser being, but because she believes her husband has a nobler job than her own.

There are good times as well: peace stations where her very own fauji will lie lazily in the backyard of the house, sipping coffee, playing with the children, while the sun sets prettily in the hills. There will also be another flavour of fauji life at another beautiful tiny station such as Umroi, with the magnificent Umiam Lake at an arm's distance before they move on to a metro like Secunderabad, where it will take her some time to accustom herself to the metro life in properly constructed accommodations, unlike the barracks she lived in before.

There could also be a time when bachelors raid her house at unearthly hours and righteously demand food.

These are the happier times for a fauji wife, but for a limited time period.

Some time ago I visited Mrs Sujata Dahiya, wife of Major Satish Dahiya, who laid down his life fighting terrorists during the Handwara operation on 14 February 2017, at her Separate Family Accommodation (SFA) at Delhi Cantonment. One step inside the house and you feel sad. The air feels gloomy, and the house is devoid of the expert touches of a decor aficionado to which an Army wife is entitled. There are no artefacts, fancy curtains, or Mhow paintings adorning the walls, but there are pictures—framed pictures—of happier times with her husband.

When I turned towards Sujata, who had been left behind, I almost didn't recognize her. She was not the same woman as in the pictures; just a shadow of the lively woman she had once been. Her eyes looked mournful and teary. There was weariness on her face, and a sense of sadness lingered about her. She did not talk much; nor did I.

These stories of couples in love being separated brutally by a violent gunfight, or a helicopter crash, or a military operation—saving the lives of others, and serving the nation—are not typical love stories of two people separated by ordinary circumstances. Here, destiny snatched their soldiers away most cruelly.

There were also times when memories of the best moments spent with him, would make the veer nari break into laughter. Her mind would flash back to the glorious days, and then to the brutal death he was fated for. And that would pluck away her peace for a long time, causing her to wake up in the middle of the night.

Broken dreams, unfulfilled promises, and feeble hopes are buried deep in the heart of such women. They have turned into a person they never thought they could be. These veer naris turn out to be a black hole of emotions, through which nothing comes out except sorrow and courage, carrying the perfect amalgamation of two contrasts. The inner turmoil sometimes blurs their vision, and they may continue to live in delusion for a long time as a wife, lover, or mother.

This was never the plan.

I met Mrs Salma Shafeeq Ghori in Bangalore. Her husband, Major Shafeeq Mahmood Khan Ghori, was killed in action on 1 July 2001. He was an Artillery officer who belonged to 172 Field Regiment, and was serving with the 30 Rashtriya Rifles in Baramulla. As a true Army officer, he ensured that his wife was a true Army wife. During their courtship period, he would send her letters, which comprised detailed descriptions of Army life and the role of an Army wife. Even after marriage, when he returned home from forward posts, the nights would be spent holding hands, and telling Salma how she needed to be brave—being an officer's wife—and how she had to fulfil her duties without worrying much about his well-being.

There was so much he had left behind, and so much she did not know.

For several months after the incident she believed it was just a bad dream, and refused to move on, until the day she realized her children, Sufia and Saif, then eight and four years old, were also in overwhelming pain. She picked herself up again. There was much paperwork to be done, and many things to wrap up, before moving house for one last time. She would take one step at a time. Their festivals and birthday celebrations halted for a long time.

She said, 'Problems were everywhere after his demise. It was like I had been left without a boat in the middle of the sea. I used to prioritize the most important issues, and had much support from his comrades who supported me all through—be it with paperwork or something else—but that was not enough. My biggest challenge was to collect myself and focus on my life ahead. The only thought that kept me moving was that I had to step into my husband's shoes somehow and perform his duties for the family we had built together, for the children he had loved so much.'

When I asked her what was so special about military love stories, she said, 'He was, is, and will always be "my forever", but I wish the society, people and the nation would acknowledge better the sacrifices of the military women who are pillars of strength for the soldiers during service and even after their death.' She paused for a moment and said, 'We sacrificed our tomorrow for your today. I hope you know this.'

Such conversations always ended with me at a loss for words. Despite being an Army wife myself, I find it difficult to talk to veer naris. How do they come out of such situations? From where do they borrow the extra courage so desperately needed to pick up the brutally shattered pieces of life? How do they acquire the expertise to manage the inconsolable children after their daddy has gone? How do they still hold the courage to live a routine life just to honour the legacy he has left behind? They are so proud of his legacy and his glory, yet it is tough to carry on. They don't know how much strength they are left with, because most of the time it feels like he has taken away everything good and happy with him.

These women go through a conflict of emotions. While trying their best to live up to the legacy, sometimes they don't realize they are braver than their men. We can never repay them for what they have done, and for what they have lost for the sake of the nation, but we surely can tell their stories to inspire future generations and raise young men and women with the right ideals. It's important for them to know how freedom is not just about guns and weapons, but more about families, emotions, ethos, and spirit.

This book is also a humble attempt to tell thousands of grieving women that they are not alone, and that we respect their sacrifices. This book could include only so many stories, but these few stories represent thousands of other women who epitomize being an Armed Forces wife.

Let these extraordinary stories begin.

The Nation Cried with Her

Lt Nitika Kaul and Major Vibhuti S. Dhoundiyal, Shaurya Chakra (P)

When the mortal remains of thirty-two-year-old Major Vibhuti Shankar Dhoundiyal were brought to his house on Nashville Road in Dehradun, Uttarakhand, on 19 February 2019, several thousand people who had assembled to pay their tributes chanted slogans in his glory: '*Major Vibhuti amar rahein! Bharat Mata ki Jai! Pakistan murdabad!* [May Major Vibhuti live forever.]' Many demonstrated against Pakistan while praising their motherland, which produces sons like Major Vibhuti.

Nitika Dhoundiyal stared at her husband's face in the coffin for a long time. She blew kisses, oblivious to the sea of people around her. The slender twenty-seven-year-old woman looked frail and crestfallen. Her head was covered in a thick shawl. Sometimes she would rest her chin against the edge of the casket, right over Vibhuti's face, and whisper something in his ears that could hear her no more. It seemed only yesterday that they had taken their wedding vows to be together for the next seven lives—and now he was gone. Death could not be the end.

It was a heartbreaking scene, one that would linger in the memory of the nation forever. Somebody tried to touch Vibhuti's face, but Nitika removed their hand immediately. It was *her* Vibhu lying there; only *hers*! As a lady officer tried to move her away from the coffin, she shouted, 'I love you, Vibhu! We all love you, but the way you loved everybody else was different because you sacrificed your life for people you never knew. You decided to lay down your life for them. You're such a brave man, and I am honoured to have you as my husband. I will love you till my last breath. I love you, Vibhu, I love you. You lied that you loved me, because you loved your nation more . . .' She turned and said, 'Let's salute this man. Jai Hind!'

Those who had gathered to pay tribute to Major Dhoundiyal watched the scene tearfully, overwhelmed by the outpouring of the young bride's grief, a woman who had become a widow only ten months after her wedding day. When they were married, Major Dhoundiyal was attached to the 55 Rashtriya Rifles (RR) and posted near Pulwama, Kashmir. After their fairytale wedding on 19 April 2018, they danced like there was no tomorrow, but he could only be with her for thirty days before rushing back to his unit. All those moments felt like a dream now. Nitika wondered for a brief moment if she was conducting herself the way her warrior husband would have expected her to, but she couldn't be sure. Perhaps it didn't matter any more.

Thousands of Indians watched Major Dhoundiyal's band of brothers in olive green fold the tricolour. Satellite channels broadcasted the cremation ceremony live. As the Shok Shastra was performed by the troops, people all over the country watched Nitika, who stood still now, her face taut with anguish, love, and unspeakable pain. Just as the Army personnel completed the last send-off, the sky opened up and the rain poured down with such urgency that it seemed as though the heavens were mourning her loss as well.

* * *

18 September 2011
Officers Training Academy,
Chennai, Tamil Nadu

The crisp morning air was bubbling with emotion and pride at the graduation parade at the OTA, Chennai. For the young men and women standing in attention, it signalled the end of the arduous year-long training programme, and the beginning of a new journey where they would soon land up in deserts, mountains, and glaciers to serve the nation.

Vibhuti Shankar Dhoundiyal was one among the 352 cadets, who took the 'Antim Pag' that day to join the Indian Army as young lieutenants. Born to Shri O.P. Dhoundiyal and Smt. Saroj Dhoundiyal on 19 February 1985, he was the youngest of four children—and the only son. And today, standing with his coterie, he watched a dream come true—a dream he had nurtured so passionately that he tried to crack the Service Selection Board (SSB) exam several times before he finally succeeded. He desperately wanted to don the olive-green uniform and serve the nation. Each time, he would remind himself of the Indian Army's recruitment campaign's tag line: 'Do You Have It in You?' And he would say, 'Yes, I have it in me!'

Vibhuti's father and grandfather had both worked in the office of the Controller, Defence Accounts. He'd had a glimpse of Defence life. As a student at the prestigious St Joseph's Academy, Dehradun, he decided that joining the Army was all he wanted in life. It would have been easy for him to give up when he couldn't pass the SSB exam more than once, but he did not quit. His failures did little to dampen his ardour and, finally, he cracked the Combined Defence Services Exam (CDSE) just after he graduated from DAV College, Dehradun.

His mates from the OTA remember his zeal and never-give-up attitude. During the course of several interviews, many of them mentioned how Vibhuti was the most jovial, happy-go-lucky member of Kohima Company. This is not to say that he didn't take his training seriously; he was at the top of his class.

Once, he fractured his leg during a rigorous exercise, and was relegated for some time, but it did not deter him an ounce and he was commissioned shortly. The injury did not stop him from achieving his goals and, soon, he was slow marching to the soulful tune of *Auld Lang Syne*, each step bringing him closer to the Antim Pag—the final step—embossed on a granite slab, marking his transformation from a cadet to an Indian Army officer, ready to face challenges to safeguard the motherland at all costs.

His seniors swear by Vibhuti's passion. He excelled in all his courses, and performed all his duties diligently. His philosophy was simple. He would tell his friends: 'Live life to the fullest because you live only once. At the end, we regret the chances we did not take.' His peers recall his catchphrase: 'Little-little.' They remember how he would say, 'Little-little *chalta hai* life *mein. Itna* serious *nahi hona* little-little *baaton pe. Chal*, little-little peg *bana*. [Things happen. You shouldn't take life too seriously. Come, serve us a drink.]'

One of his course mates, Major Sunil Kumar M.V., who was with him in Kohima Company, said, 'He had a very positive attitude towards everything. He would crack jokes during the toughest of tasks, make people laugh when they felt alone. He was always full of life, and equally passionate about his training. Trust me, you need to be highly motivated to fall and rise with equal enthusiasm, but that is how he was. Vibhuti never knew how to give up. I remember his whole family came for the pipping ceremony. His father looked especially proud.'

It had rained the night before the ceremony, and the Major Parameshwaran Drill Square inside the OTA was completely wet. But nothing could dampen the collective mood of the smart and energetic young men and women, or prevent them from taking their Antim Pag. That was a happy day when Vibhuti's proud sisters, and his mother and father flanked his side 'pipping' the well-deserved stars on his uniform.

As is the norm with service officers, Lieutenant Dhoundiyal was attached to an infantry unit, 17 Mahar, based at Nangi Tekri in the Krishna Ghati sector in Poonch District, near the LoC. It was a sensitive area where heavy shelling, regular infiltrations, and ceasefire violations were routine.

The first posting is always special and leaves an everlasting impression on the young officers' minds. It was where Captain Dhoundiyal imbibed the Mahar Regiment's war cry, '*Bolo Hindustan ki jai!*', and decided his professional goals. This was why he pursued various ambitious Army courses from 2013 to 2017 from the premium Army institutes in India. In his eight-year-long service life, he achieved laurels soldiers worked their entire careers to attain. After his Kashmir tenure, he was sent to Rajasthan, Pune, and Secundrabad on various postings and military courses. The courses provided him with an upper hand in strategy formation and decision-making while leading the troops. They taught him to not just be a soldier, but also a leader his men would look up to.

From 2011–17, he steadily rose through the ranks and, in 2018, Major Dhoundiyal was an EME (Electrical and Mechanical Engineering) officer deputed to the 55 Rashtriya Rifles, a specialized counter-insurgency force deployed in Pulwama, Kashmir.

* * *

December 2015
Chandigarh

Nitika had finally agreed to meet Captain Dhoundiyal at the Rock Garden in Chandigarh. At that time she was pursuing her MBA from Panjab University. She had known him from when she was studying for her BTech degree in Electronics and Communication at Manav Rachna College of Engineering in Faridabad, Haryana. They had been introduced by mutual friends. The young officer was pursuing a degree in Engineering at the College of Military Engineering, Pune, and their first interaction was followed by a Facebook friend request—and several messages on it from Vibhuti's side. He was pursuing her and made no bones about it. She, on the other hand, was almost indifferent to him, busy studying.

But people destined to be together will meet anyway. When Vibhuti happened to visit Chandigarh by chance, he requested Nitika to meet him and she agreed. There was something about him that intrigued her. They decided to meet at the Rock Garden on 12 December 2015.

That day, the Rock Garden was celebrating a festival to mark its creator Nek Chand Saini's birth anniversary, and the place was buzzing with activity. The Garden was like a fantasy land comprising thousands of sculptures made from debris, stones, and discarded junk. Vibhuti and Nitika felt as if they had slid into the labyrinthine interiors of a man's incredible imagination.

The place was full of tram rides, slides, camel rides, and swings. Nitika swayed on the swings with a sparkle in her eyes; her childlike enthusiasm captivated Vibhuti. It was so unlike the rough-and-tough life he led as a fauji. His life back at the OTA mostly comprised tough physical exercises. Her easy, full-throated laughter and delight in small things amused him; he'd never met anyone like her.

'At the end of the day, just before leaving the park, we came across concave and convex mirrors, the ones that distort body shapes, show long faces, project an image with four hands or a protruding tummy, and display other funny figures. The mirror changed our appearance as well, and made me look fat. Vibhu started teasing me. "*Chalo yaar*, reality *mein na sahi, kam se kam* mirror *mein khud ko moti dekh ke khush ho jao*! [Come, see yourself as fat in a mirror—if not in reality—and be happy.]" I stared at him in mock anger, and the next second we broke into hysterical laughter. It was a beautiful day—the first of many magical meetings we had during our courtship period,' Nitika recalled in one of our interviews for this book.

A few days after their date at the Rock Garden, she uploaded a picture on Facebook, but edited him out. Vibhuti was upset and commented on the photo: 'Why did you crop out the boy beside you? Did you not like me?' Nitika's face broke into a wide smile when she read that. In that moment she knew he was the one. She had never come across such a straightforward and sincere man. The simplicity and consistency of his proposals made her lose her heart to him. Little did she know that it would soon change the course of her life in a way she could never have imagined.

* * *

19 April 2018
Faridabad

The intricate arrangement of marigolds at the wedding hall, the peachy drapes with fairy lights, the floral arrangements and foliage accents had transformed the ordinary marriage hall into a miniature heaven on earth. Buffet tables groaned under the weight of mounds of food displayed on beautifully decorated plates. Even the smaller ceremonies—haldi, sangeet, mehendi—were performed extravagantly. After all, Vibhuti and Nitika were getting married, an event Major Dhoundiyal's mother and sisters had waited for, for so long. Nitika could not stop blushing. Her insistence had forced the usually rational soldier to get married during his tenure with the Rashtriya Rifles in Kashmir. Everybody, including their friends, had advised them against it, asking them to wait until the period ended. Even a month before the wedding, Vibhuti was hesitant. He said, 'Nikki, life is risky there, and there are uncertainties. I think we should wait.'

Nitika replied, 'Vibhu, the biggest risk in life is not taking any risks. Don't you think everything in life is a risk? I mean, you walk out onto the street—and it is a risk. But spending every second with you as your wife will be worth it for me. *Chadd na yaar, karte hain!* [Come on, let's do it!]'

And just like that, it was decided that they would be married as soon as Vibhuti had leave. Their families got along famously when they met over several cups of tea and plates of samosas. They bonded over family values and, soon, were laughing over little inside jokes.

The date 19 April was chosen for the wedding. At this time, Major Dhoundiyal had taken over as the Delta Company Commander in 55 Rastriya Rifles. He put his heart and soul into training his men for the many successful operations to come. He was granted a month's leave. He had had this inexplicable desire to get married at a time when everybody else would have opted to do it after the risky tenure was over. It's hard to reason out why. For Vibhuti, perhaps marrying Nitika was already written in the stars. Perhaps the universe wanted him to live, love, and experience everything in what was to be a short but extraordinary life.

The wedding ceremony began with a three-hour-long wait for the baraat with endless dancing. The groom arrived in a fancy vintage car, and the bride walked in with her family and friends under a canopy of flowers. Everyone, from the guests to the groom, had waited impatiently for the first glimpse of the bride. Nitika walked down the aisle to the tune of 'Din Shagna Da', looking resplendent in her orange lehenga. Chunky bangles, maang tikka, a necklace, and statement earrings highlighted her natural beauty. Vibhuti looked dapper in a cream and golden sherwani, teamed up with a maroon saafa. The smiles on their faces didn't disappear even when the pandit recited the shlokas, talking about a relationship that would span seven lives. Theirs was undoubtedly one such. The wedding soiree was a delightful event for all the guests.

At their reception, the fairytale couple took to the dance floor for their wedding waltz. Nitika was giddy with happiness. Endless strings of lights covering the ceiling, along with thousands of fairy lights entwined together made it seem as if they were dancing under a starlit sky. Dressed in a maroon lehenga with minimal make-up, Nitika was a sight to behold. Vibhuti could not stop gushing over his bride.

Looking around him, he felt that his life was finally complete. He could see how happy his mother, Saroj, looked. It had been long since he had seen her smile like that after he lost his father in 2012. He could see how his sisters and Nitika were bonding, and their vibrant happy laughter over silly jokes filled his heart.

But his month-long leave vanished in a heartbeat. Even as he was boarding his flight for Srinagar, it seemed as though he had landed in Dehradun only yesterday. It was tough leaving Nitika behind, but he forced himself to ignore her tear-filled eyes. He didn't have the luxury to stay back when duty was calling.

His colleagues still remember he threw a lavish party for all his comrades as soon as he returned to his unit. One of his close friends said, 'All the food was catered from Srinagar. In RR, it is difficult to get food from outside, but he did everything to throw us an excellent party. He was elated.'

* * *

13 October 2018
Dalipora, Pulwama
3.00 a.m.
Major Dhoundiyal was initially posted as the Officer Commanding, Field Repair Increment, which acted as a tech support sub-unit to the 55 Rashtriya Rifles. However, his daredevil attitude, willingness to take risks, and excellent performance pushed the Commanding Officer to appoint him as the Company Commander of Delta Company, where his role was to lead field operations and encounters.

It proved to be a great decision eventually, and added to the glory of the 55 Rashtriya Rifles, especially after the encounter with the mastermind behind the Pulwama attack, Pakistani terrorist Abdul Rasheed Ghazi.

Major Dhoundiyal put his entire effort into running Delta Company. He would personally ensure that the morale of his men was always high. The operational preparedness would be his top priority, and many a time he would participate in the interrogations. He gradually built up a string of reliable informants in the local area. Soon Delta Company got its first major breakthrough when the Para Special Forces operatives from the neighbouring units provided him with input regarding Lashkar-e-Taiba (LeT) militants hiding in Dalipora, which fell under his area.

It was around 3.00 a.m., and the air was chilly when Major Dhoundiyal launched the cordon-and-search operation in the area to track down the militants. Two separate cordons—inner and outer—covering the entire area were laid out, but they heard sounds of firing from outside the cordons. Everybody else expected the terrorists to escape, but Major Dhoundiyal's instincts told him otherwise. He continued with his search. It was only when he, along with his buddy, and a non-commissioned officer (NCO) from the Quick Response Team (QRT) reached the kitchen garden that they spotted the terrorist, Shabir Ahmad Dar of Lashkar-e-Taiba, hiding in the hedge. All three fired their guns before Dar could retaliate.

Shabir Ahmad Dar was killed, while another militant—Showkat Ahmad Dar—sustained a bullet injury and was shifted to Shri Maharaja Hari Singh hospital in

Srinagar after the police officials and the CRPF personnel had joined the operation. By 6.40 a.m. the stone-pelters gathered—local Kashmiris—protesting against the Indian Army. However, by then the operation had already been called off. That also speaks volumes about the tactical brilliance of the Indian Army.

Another officer, who was a part of the operations, later shared more details with me. He said, 'It was a huge success for Delta Company. The boys were thrilled. It was their first contact after a long time. Certainly a big moment for the company and also the unit. It had always had competent Company Commanders, but they had missed out on several opportunities to shine. It was only when Major Dhoundiyal took over that luck favoured them, or maybe it was just his instincts that always led him to the right spot. He produced results. We could also see how diligently he would push his boys to prepare hard.' It was just the beginning of Major Dhoundiyal's short but illustrious career in the Indian Army.

* * *

10 November 2018
Tikken Batpora, Pulwama
South Kashmir

Major Dhoundiyal, the Delta Company Commander of 55 Rashtriya Rifles, had been meticulously searching houses along with the Foxtrot Company Commander, a senior officer, and was in charge of the whole operation. It was

5.30 a.m. when they received conclusive information and cordoned off the Tikken village.

The weather was extreme—the cold wave in Kashmir had recently intensified—and heavy snowfall gripped the Valley. But the tip-off regarding two Hizb-ul-Mujahideen terrorists, Liaqat Munir Wani and Wajid Ul Islam, was of high priority. Both identified as second-generation terrorists, were wanted over a series of ambushes they had carried out on the security forces. They had also attacked many civilians. There were many FIRs registered against their names.

Three separate cordons were laid out in the area. The security forces knocked the door at each house. By 7:30 a.m. they had searched about a hundred houses, which was a Herculean task. At that point Major Dhoundiyal found two houses in a single compound and, when he knocked on the door, nobody responded. Eventually, when the door opened, they found four women inside, two of whom were foreigners and were speaking in Punjabi urdu as spoken in Pakistan than the usual Kashmiri language. Major Dhoundiyal grew suspicious, and carried out an extensive search of the building.

One of the soldiers from his squad said, 'There was a point when we stopped believing that the terrorists were still in the area. The troops whispered about how the tip-off was a hoax. But it was the sheer brilliance of Vibhuti Sir that he carried out an excellent search of the house, going through places one might have missed. It was he who found a mobile cover in the chimney, and told us it could not be right. Then he located fake military boots smeared with fresh snow hidden in one of the corners.'

Immediately, Major Dhoundiyal informed the Foxtrot Company Commander. The experienced Company Commander laid a brilliant trap. While Major Dhoundiyal, with his Company, climbed over the roof to provide an aerial cover for the ground troops, the Commander started taking rounds of the house. When he reached the lawn, the terrorists hiding under some grass suddenly revealed themselves and opened fire on him. Always alert, Major Dhoundiyal fired back at them, and the Foxtrot Company Commander, who got enough time to take cover, also started firing from the ground. The terrorists were now well and truly trapped, and soon they were shot dead.

It was a hugely successful operation, and one for which the Commanding Officer recommended Major Vibhuti for his first Gallantry Award. Returning to his unit, Vibhuti was given a hero's welcome, and the entire unit partied all night. The CO 55 RR also joined them.

His junior, who also shared a room with him, recalled those times. During his interview with me he said excitedly, 'Vibhuti Sir was an excellent snooker player—the best. No one—I repeat no one—could ever beat him at it. Snooker was our game for victory parties, and that night he played like never before. We all played against him, and he knocked us out easily. Each time he won, he would shout triumphantly. After some time, we stopped playing with him, and he kept teasing us about it for a long time.'

The brothers-in-arms shared jokes along with drinks, laughed, and danced, and they loudly cheered to more operational success. The morale of Delta Company was at an all-time high.

* * *

January 2019
Faridabad

Vibhuti was on leave for a month. He wanted to celebrate the new year with his wife. At the time, Nitika was working with the prestigious Tata Consultancy Services as a business analyst. Vibhuti's beard had grown, a change from his usually clean-shaven face. Suddenly, he looked mature to Nitika. Instead of cracking jokes, he would now talk about life and death.

Nitika remembers his mood. While speaking to me she said, 'Though he never shared the details of his operations, he was aware of the high-risk, life-threatening situations he was involved in. Many a time he tried to tell me to be strong and tough, like an Army wife should be. I would not take it seriously then, but now I feel his deep concern and affection behind those words.'

One night, Vibhuti held her hands and said, 'Nikki, you know I am a very happy man. I feel I have achieved everything in life, and I have absolutely no regrets. But you know what, *aagar mai tumse baat kiye bina shaheed ho gaya to iska mujhe afsos hoga.* [I don't think I could ever be at peace if I die without talking to you for one last time.]'

Nitika was shaken and distraught. He was saying things no newly married woman wanted to hear. He was also voicing her worst fears. She replied, 'Please don't talk like that. How dare you!'

Major Dhoundiyal didn't have the heart to tell her what he already knew about his job. Life in the Rashtriya

Rifles was not only risky, but also unpredictable. He had watched his comrades die on the battlefield. Some of them had been the most skilled officers, but they too could not fight their fate. There had been times when a fraction of a second had saved him, but there was no way he could say all those things to his wife. He had not even been able to stay with her long enough because of his RR tenure, and he knew how eagerly she was waiting for it to end in January the next year. They had plans.

Immediately, Major Dhoundiyal apologized. 'Okay Baba! Sorry. *Lo kaan pakad liya. Khush abhi*? [Look, I apologized. Are you happy now?]' Nitika rolled her eyes, furrowed her eyebrows in mock anger, brought her face near his and said '*Thodi si*. [Yes, a little.]' She giggled heartily. The moment of tension had passed.

Major Dhoundiyal took her in his arms. 'On a serious note, Nikki,' he said, 'I want you to work harder and carve a position for yourself in your organization. Your aim should always be to achieve more, and never settle for what you have today. Failure should never scare you.'

Nitika replied, 'I am working hard, Vibhu—giving my best to my company—but I don't know whether I want to continue with my job once you are back from RR. I am looking forward to Army life too. I have heard it is a little busy for most wives, and there are many commitments to fulfil. I don't know whether I will be able to strike a balance between my professional and Army lives.'

Major Dhoundiyal said, 'Don't worry. We will find a way. I will request for a posting with you. We will hire more support and make it work, but you never have to give up on your career even if I am not around. It is crucial that you stand on your feet.'

Nitika was perturbed when she heard him say that. 'What do you mean by "even if I am not around?"'

He smiled. '*Arre Baba!* I just mean . . . don't stop or quit anything for anyone. Always keep moving. This is the only way forward. Life is a gift. This is the only thing I ask of you. No matter what, you will always find me standing beside you wherever you are.'

The floral curtains billowed with the breeze, and the twinkling fairy lights filled the room with hope and warmth. She was proud to have a progressive man as her life partner. It was his encouragement that had always pushed her to achieve more. Her eyes shone with immense gratitude. How lucky she was!

She ruffled Vibhuti's hair gently as he slept in peace. How she wished for time to stop right there. She was aware he was to leave soon. His absence always made her very lonely, and she tried to ward it off by immersing herself in work, but it was tough. She dreamt of starting a family soon.

After a few days Nitika waved him goodbye with a heavy heart, but with a smile on her face. It was always difficult. There was still so much left to talk about, to laugh about, to celebrate together, but she knew he was duty-bound. His nation and job would always come first. And was she not proud? She sure was.

Vibhuti was her whole world. He offered her true love, and showed her its power to change lives. She was in college when they first met, dealing with acne and low self-esteem.

She would undergo intense treatments, and later writhe in agony while her skin recovered. Vibhuti had been a friend then. There were no commitments, nothing.

He once said to her, 'Nitika, you need to understand that if somebody loves you, your pimples won't deter him. Love is a tremendous feeling, and your imperfections are insignificant for those who love you. Let them be. Don't change yourself.'

Nitika was deeply moved by his little speech. He was right. She had always tried to please others. Those words proved magical, and almost instantly she was freed from the urge to please people or prove her worth to them. Overnight she felt comfortable in her skin. The new-found confidence helped her take on new challenges, and she always acknowledged Vibhuti's role in helping her succeed.

Now that he is gone, sometimes it becomes confusing for her when she comes across an obstacle. There is no shoulder to lean on, no hand to hold, and no heart that understands hers. She doesn't know whom to turn to. She feels Vibhuti all around her, shining high in the sky and lingering in her dreams. It brings a smile to her face and hope in her heart.

She said to me, 'I don't know why, but remembering him does not make me sad. He has only given me happy memories. There is nothing to cry about. No doubt my loss can never be compensated, and the pain is real, but he bestowed a lot of positivity and happiness upon me, and I want to keep it like that. After all, my husband was a Braveheart; how can I ever fall or stumble?'

* * *

6 February 2019
Chakoora, Pulwama
Kashmir

Kashmir, Paradise on Earth, was at its coldest. The entire Valley was covered in a blanket of snow. An intense cold wave in the Valley had dropped the minimum temperatures to below the freezing point. Vibhuti would tell Nitika how he would have loved having a cup of hot tea with her in such weather. He loved Kashmir. Over the years he had grown fond of the land, which provided him with a glimpse of impossible beauty, strife, and sacrifice. And he was thankful for it.

It was raining heavily the day Major Dhoundiyal received a piece of information in the afternoon—it required timely action. His source told him that Lashkar-e-Taiban terrorists, including the District Commander—Irfan Ahmad Sheikh—would be moving outside the area in half an hour. Vibhuti was smiling when he left with his QRT. He knew terrorists always sought the cover of such weather. The tip-off meant he did not have time for preparation, but it did not matter to him. He valued his resources, and knew the right information at the right time was pivotal for the fight against terrorism.

As he was laying the cordon in the area, he found the terrorists boarding a civil vehicle in a bid to escape. The terrorists began firing at him and his men. Vibhuti and his QRT immediately fired back. They could not board their vehicles, and started running on foot. Vibhuti set off on a chase. The terrorists ran into a field and fired at them. The Forces retaliated. Vibhuti kept shouting instructions to his men. Meanwhile, the news reached the Commanding Officer, and an outer cordon was also thrown round Chakoora village in the Litter area of Pulwama District.

The big nallahs in Kashmir served as an easy escape route for the terrorists, and they jumped into it. Major Dhoundiyal was determined not to let them get away so quickly. He also jumped in after them. It was not only risky, but also suicidal. The water rose to their waist, but Major Dhoundiyal did not give up, and eventually shot down Irfan Ahmad Sheikh— later identified as the District Commander of Lashkar-e-Taiba. The encounter took place amid a torrential downpour, and the soldiers with Major Dhoundiyal describe that chase as straight out of a Bollywood movie. One AK-47 rifle and two magazines were recovered from the encounter site. Another militant took advantage of the shootout and fled from the village. Sheikh's body, drenched in blood and mud, went viral on social media after the encounter.[1]

It was not even a week later that the Pulwama attack shook the nation. The sheer audacity of Adil Ahmad Dar, a local Kashmiri militant who rammed an SUV carrying around 60 kg of explosives into the CRPF convoy, resulting in a massive explosion that cost forty brave CRPF soldiers their lives, was difficult to comprehend. He was a sucide bomber from Jaish-e-Mohammed (JeM), who died in the blast himself, but the impact of this explosion not only destroyed forty families but also shook the very core of India. The entire nation stood together against terrorism. Revenge could not wait.

* * *

17 February 2019
Pulwama

Major Dhoundiyal called his wife late that night. He did not know that it would be the last time he would speak to her. He knew Nitika was worried after the Pulwama attack, even though she never expressed her emotions. It was their code of conduct: Vibhuti never complained about his work conditions, and she never said she was fearful on his behalf.

She once shared her feelings with me. She said, 'He was already burdened with a lot of things, and I never wanted him to worry about me too. His job was risky. I would always tell him not to fret. I supported the rest of the family and they supported me, so that he could focus completely on his job. But yes, he knew I was waiting for him eagerly, and that he should come back to me as early as possible. I would count the days back then, without realizing that the counting would last for eternity.'

She knew Vibhuti had lost his father in 2012, not long after his commissioning from OTA, Chennai, in September 2011, and that he worried about his mother and his sisters. She always tried her best to do her bit, not just as a daughter-in-law but also as a daughter.

Over their last call they discussed their first wedding-anniversary plans, before bidding each other goodbye. The end was only a few hours away, ready to rob them of everything they had hoped for and dreamt of.

Vibhuti was to visit Dehradun for their first marriage anniversary in April 2019, and every day Nitika and he would plan the celebrations. One of his sisters lived in the

US, and she too was supposed to visit them. They would discuss the venue, menu, guest list, and more. Nitika was unaware that his sisters had planned to surprise them by framing their wedding pictures and putting them all over their house in Dehradun.

* * *

18 February 2019
Pinglana, Pulwama

The nation was still mourning the deaths of the forty-four CRPF personnel in Pulwama on 14 February 2019. The severity of the Pakistan-backed attack caused the Indian Government to scrap off the status of the 'most favoured nation' from Pakistan immediately. The status had provided them a non-discriminatory access to the Indian markets and export goods, at low custom duty. In addition, the Indian Army also launched one of the most extensive cordon-and-search operations in the area. The boys were eager to avenge their dead comrades.

The 55 Rashtriya Rifles had received some general information from the central intelligence agencies, regarding the presence of Jaish-e-Mohammed (JeM) terrorists in their area. The Chief Operational Commander of JeM in the area, Abdul Rashid Gazi aka Kamran, a Pakistani national, was hiding in the Pinglana region. He was the mastermind behind the Pulwama terror attack. Though the information was very vague, and meant that a huge area had to be prepared for the cordon-and-search operation at a battalion level, involving more men, the security agencies were unwilling to let Kamran escape.

Major Dhoundiyal knew that if Kamran gave them the slip this time, they would never be able to catch him. They received the tip-off at around 7.00 p.m. and the Companies moved soon after. Major Dhoundiyal planned a battalion-level cordon-and-search operation meticulously. The Companies spread out in the area with an equal number of QRTs. It appeared as though the cordon was only laid out from one side and the other side had been kept light. This was a strategic decision. It was on the seemingly lighter side that Major Dhoundiyal laid his trap along with his QRT. A targeted operation was launched, and all parties began searching the houses in the Pinglana area. The weather was especially bad that day. The fog had intensified, resulting in poor visibility. Cold winds whiplashed their faces.

Major Dhoundiyal found a cluster of houses. When he entered the third one, he found a few suspicious things thrown in the space between the two boundary walls of the adjacent houses. 'Perhaps the terrorists were trying to shift houses because the house owner had not informed the forces, the way they usually do. Most of the time, the house owner is aware of terrorists hiding on their premises, and they run away so that they are not caught in the middle of a gunfight. However, this unfortunate house owner was perhaps not aware of this, which eventually cost him his life. He was the only civilian casualty,' an officer involved in the operation recounted on the condition of anonymity.

Major Dhoundiyal's radar was on high alert—he immediately radioed the other Company Commander.

He said, 'Search *chal rahi hai. Main ghar ke ander jaa raha hoon*, civilians *ko bahar baitha diya hai*, house owner *ko kuch nahi pata. Tum* search *kar rahe ho na . . . samajh rahe ho na . . . Sabhi ko bata dena.* [The search is on. I'm going in. The civilians are outside. The house owner knows nothing. I hope you're still searching, and I hope you understand. Tell everyone.] Over and Out!'

It was around 1.00 a.m., and the darkness made things even more difficult. In the lull before the storm, Major Dhoundiyal, along with five other members of his QRT, searched the house in question extensively. It was when they moved to the back of the building that his fellow soldier, Sepoy Hari Singh, said, '*Saab, udhar dekho kuch pairo ke nishan se dikh rahe hain.* [Saheb, look, you can see some footprints there.]'

They had no cover, and they could have waited for the backup, but the footprints on the fresh snow indicated that someone had just moved to the other side of the house where the cattle were kept. They could not afford to wait; it could mean losing Kamran and his men. They moved towards that side immediately, with Major Dhoundiyal leading his men from the front.

When they moved closer to the cattle shed, the terrorists suddenly opened fire on them. The militants were aware of the Force's movements, and they had strategically chosen the cattle shed as a vantage point to launch their attack. Major Dhoundiyal bore the brunt of the first round of gunfire. He was shot multiple times. His men were also wounded. He retaliated instantly, and pushed his men behind, disregarding his own safety. He then crawled to the animal shed, in the line of fire, to launch what would be his final attack.

Major Dhoundiyal knew it was a death trap. He was severely injured, but he didn't lose his composure even though he could probably feel his life slipping away from him. Without backing down, he and his men kept firing at the terrorists, waiting for the moment when the enemy would slip up. And they did. One of the terrorists moved out of the shed, firing in all directions, as he tried to escape. Major Dhoundiyal had one shot, and he took it, bringing the enemy down. In a desperate attempt to flee, the remaining terrorists threw a grenade that killed Vibhuti's entire team except for one soldier who managed to crawl back to rest of the battalion and apprised them of the situation.

By the time the evacuation team arrived, the remaining terrorists had fled. Another officer junior to Vibhuti, his close friend and roommate, took over the operation that went on for seventeen hours straight and finished the next evening. A second terrorist, Hilal Ahmad, a bomb specialist and a local recruited by JeM, was also killed. The next evening, another was eliminated. The operation wiped out the top leadership of the JeM in the Valley.[2]

Major Vibhuti Shankar Dhoundiyal, along with his trusted brothers from his beloved Delta Company, Havaldar Sheo Ram, Sepoy Hari Singh, and Sepoy Ajay Kumar, made the supreme sacrifice in the line of duty. Police Head Constable, Abdul Rashid Kalas, was also killed in action in the same operation and immortalized himself. Amit Kumar, DIG South Kashmir, also sustained minor bullet injuries at the same time.

Several weapons, including an AK-47 rifle, and a pistol, were recovered from the site of the encounter. That evening, Pakistan bombarded the Indian side of Kashmir with mortar and artillery fire. The enemy was angry, and they wanted to hit back in whichever way they could.

Lieutenant Gen. Kanwal Jeet Singh Dhillon, Corps Commander, Chinar Corps, in Srinagar, stated to the press after the successful completion of the operation: 'We did not want civilian casualties. As you are aware, other than one civilian casualty, which happened due to terrorist fire in the initial stages itself, not a single civilian has been injured in this operation that lasted seventeen hours. That is the risk we took, and we took it on our chin.'

Major Dhoundiyal took his last breath around 2.00 a.m. His mission had been successful. He had eliminated a major terrorist—Abdul Rasheed Ghazi, aka Kamran—one of the closest and most trusted aides of the Jaish-e-Mohammed chief, Maulana Masood Azhar.[3]

As part of the bigger plan, Rasheed had crossed the LoC in December 2018 after dodging the Army, and started operating in Pulwama. His prime job was to radicalize, recruit, and train locals for militancy, while working on the larger plan to cause massive havoc. The Afghan War veteran was a bomb specialist, and he trained several local militants to make and detonate bombs. Adil Dar, the young Kashmiri militant, who was eventually selected for the Pulwama attack, was one among them. Had it not been for Major Dhoundiyal, a terrorist Commander like Kamran would have been a threat not only to the local peace but also to national security. His early killing in the encounter by Major Dhoundiyal halted many terror plots, and disrupted the local terrorists' network completely.

* * *

19 February 2019
Dehradun

Life is nothing but a series of strange coincidences, thought Nitika. It was bizarre how the love of her life had made the supreme sacrifice in a place her family had once called home. She was born in Faridabad in 1991, after her Kashmiri Pandit family migrated from Kashmir in 1990, in search of peace and a new life. 'That piece of land has taken so much from me—almost everything,' she said during her interview. She was destined to be part of its history in the most dignified manner possible. Why only her, thousands of women who have lost their fathers, brothers, sons, and husbands to terrorism that has ravaged the state, are equally significant in the state's historical records.

Nitika left for Dehradun as soon as she received the news. She was in shock. It was unbelievable. Vibhuti was supposed to visit her in April for their first wedding anniversary. It felt as though her world had ended in a single moment.

And though she was devastated, she worried about conveying the news to her mother-in-law. Vibhu had been her only son and the light of her life. Nitika knew people had told Saroj only that Vibhuti was injured; she knew her mother-in-law must be beside herself with worry.

When Nitika met her, she tried her best to control her tears. The moment Saroj saw her, she rushed towards her, hugged her tightly, and asked about her well-being.

That was it. Barriers were broken, and the two women closest of all to the slain hero—the one who had birthed him and raised him, and the one who had dreamt of a world with him—cried till they could cry no more. Vibhuti's sisters sobbed in the other corner. Their tears have not dried yet. The pain of losing their only brother, whom they eagerly waited to tie a rakhi to, or pamper, has been too much to bear. Saroj did not crumble after her husband's demise, but the untimely death of her son, whom she had conceived after many prayers, broke her heart.

Nitika's parents reached Dehradun, and they too were shattered. Major Dhoundiyal had been like a son to them. Now they had to see their beloved daughter as a widow wilting with grief. For it was only yesterday, wasn't it, when they had married her off to Vibhuti with great joy?

When the pyre was lit, the blaze ate away at the happiness and hopes of two families. People watching the funeral on their TV screens, all over India, cried along with the woman who had lost her entire world in a cruel, decisive moment—one that had also filled the hearts of her countrymen and women with pride.

* * *

By the time you read this, Dear reader, Nitika has joined the Indian Army in the Army Ordnance Corps. During the SSB interview she was asked, 'Why do you want to join the Indian Army?' She told the interviewers about Major Dhoundiyal, and said, 'I want to complete the rest of the tenure of my husband, and take his legacy forward.'

When asked how long she had been married to Major Dhoundiyal, she said, 'Around a year and half-a-month.' One of the officers objected to her response. He said, 'How can you say so? According to the records, Major Dhoundiyal was killed in action within nine months and twenty-nine days of your marriage.'

Without batting an eyelid Nitika replied with grace and confidence, 'I lost him, but that does not mean our marriage ended. He has just gone to the other side, and it's not like we got a divorce or I have remarried. You see, I am still married to him.'

If you ever wonder about the source of strength in our men in uniform who willingly face bullets, cross bridges, face the blasts, and risk their lives boldly, remember that these women are braver. They serve as a huge source of inspiration and motivation to them.

Nitika's reply made the interview panel smile. When the results were out, she was recommended. This news made many headlines in the national media, for she serves as a huge inspiration to India's youth, especially young women.

Her date of joining her duty was delayed because of the Covid-19 outbreak in 2020 but, as soon as she received it, she headed to the OTA, Chennai, with the same black trunk Major Vibhuti Dhoundiyal had used during his training at the OTA. The trunk had been repainted just like her life. After a year-long training programme, on

29 May 2021, Nitika marched alongside her course mates on the same grounds of Major Parameshwaran Drill Square at the OTA, Chennai, where her husband had marched in 2011. She was pipped by the Parade Reviewing Officer, Lt Gen. Y.K. Joshi, General Officer Commanding-in-Chief (GOC-in-C), Northern Command, himself, who displayed the highest military code of conduct, and principles, by supporting the wife of a brother officer who took his last breath in the Northern Command. Regimental accoutrements and bright shiny stars, provided a glorious aura to the newly commissioned Lieutenant Nitika Kaul Dhoundiyal—about to start the new chapter of her life.

Dear reader, through her story I hope you will realize that true love does not weaken you; rather it provides the power to conquer all. All you need to do is to believe in the power of love.

* * *

The story has been written based on the interviews with Mrs Nitika Dhoundiyal, wife of Major Vibhuti Shankar Dhoundiyal; Major Dhoundiyal's course mates, officers and other men, namely Captain Saurabh Patni, Major Vipul Narayanan, and Major Sunil, who were with him during his training at the Academy, postings, and various operations. For displaying conspicuous bravery and unparalleled courage resulting in the elimination of a deadly terrorist, Major Vibhuti Shankar Dhoundiyal was awarded the Shaurya Chakra posthumously.[4]

An Eternal Love Story

Trupti Nair and
Major Shashidharan Vijay Nair

Vaikunth Smashanbhoomi
Pune, Maharashtra
13 January 2019

Thousands and thousands of people had gathered at Vaikunth Crematorium in Navi Peth, Pune, Maharashtra, to pay their respects and mourn the martyrdom of Pune's son, Major Shashidharan Vijay Nair. He had sacrificed his life trying to save other people in an improvised explosive device (IED) blast at the beautiful Lam Valley in Nowshera, Jammu and Kashmir.

It was an emotional adieu, the kind that suited the stature of an immortal who has sacrificed his life for the nation. Thousands mourned the death of the legend who had never backed out from a single responsibility. He had led his life selflessly for other people, the nation, and his family. There was not an inch of space left where people were not standing. All three floors of the crematorium were filled by a massive crowd that had also occupied nearby buildings. They wanted to pay their last tribute to Major Nair, the son of the nation—a Malayali by origin, but a Marathi by heart, and a Gorkha in spirit. After he attained martyrdom on Friday, 11 January 2019, his body, wrapped in tricolour and put into a casket, had reached Pune with state honours. Six service aircrafts had been used to transport his mortal remains to his home town—a rare honour.

After the ceremonial guard of honour, his body was kept in the morgue. The journey to the funeral home began at 10.00 a.m. in the form of an enormous procession attended by thousands of people from all across the nation. Most shopkeepers on the procession's route had downed their shutters in his memory. Hoardings were placed, and makeshift tents were erected overnight, to accommodate the thousands who had gathered.

Vehicular traffic was also stopped at Singhad Road. Police personnel were posted everywhere. They would salute his mortal remains on the army truck bedecked with flowers, before halting the traffic to give way to the hero's funeral procession. The residents would shower flowers on the truck. Hundreds of youth followed the procession with a tiranga in their hands. The slogans chanted in the glory of Major Shashidharan Nair pierced the sky. That continued throughout the 18 km-journey from Khadakwasla to Vaikunth Crematorium, till the crowd halted for the last rites, and the family members placed the floral wreath on the Major's body.

Full state honours and 21-Gun salutes were given to the brave son of the soil. His twelve-year-old cousin, Ashvat, who had come from Kerala especially for this, lit the funeral pyre. There wasn't a single hand that did not salute Major Nair's valour, before his body burnt to ashes and he became one with the same soil for which he had sacrificed his life.

Amid the mourning crowd, on a wheelchair, sat a solitary woman who had suffered the most significant loss of them all—his wife, Trupti. Beside her stood Major Nair's mother, Mrs Lata Nair, who had lost her own husband several years ago, and was now mourning the loss of her son. There also stood Sheena Nair, Major Nair's sister, grieving her brother's sudden demise. She was uncertain about whom she should hold—her sick mother, who had been released from the hospital the night before, or her sister-in-law, Trupti—sitting transfixed on her wheelchair, crushed by the unimaginable loss of her pillar of strength.

Trupti's misfortune was hard to ignore. Soon, her story made headlines in every newspaper and on every media channel. The journalists were astonished at the intensity of her relationship with Major Nair.

People like him appear among us only to spread great light in this dark world filled with lies and miseries. They set torches of hope, love, and purity, blazing to guide the others. At first you may think such men of honour and dignity don't exist any more but, as you gradually read their stories, your faith in humanity and goodness will be restored. Such is the story of Major Shashidharan Vijay Nair and the woman in his life.

* * *

2003
Fergusson College
Pune
Maharashtra

A tall and brawny eighteen-year-old, carrying a bag on his back, pedalled his bicycle vigorously at 5.00 a.m. to reach Fergusson College, 20 km away from his home in Khadakwasla on the outskirts of Pune.

It was his daily routine. Shashidharan Vijay Nair would pedal his bicycle for around 40 km a day to attend college, mostly because of two reasons. First, he had an aptitude for Army training, and was very punctual in attending his NCC classes and physical drills early in the morning. Second, he did not belong to a financially secure family. The sole income for his family came from the tuitions his mother, Lata, provided. His father had taken voluntary retirement from Central Water & Power Research Station because of ill health.

Shashidharan knew he was meant to don the olive-green uniform. This was why he chose the Army wing of his college, the NCC, as part of the batch of 2006. He proved to be the best cadet of his batch, the best athlete, a great cross-country runner, one of the best basketball players, and more. He remained invincible in all the physical exercises given to him.

One of his childhood friends, who was in the NCC with him and later joined the Army, Major Milind Kulkarni, remembers him fondly. During our conversation he said, 'We had a pagoda-shaped structure at the top of the hill behind our college grounds. All the NCC cadets would gather and warm up for the day by climbing up to it and touching it. By the time we started ascending, Shashi would be returning down the slope. This resulted in extra drills and punishments for the rest of us. We would surround him later and ask him to slow down for our sake: "*Thoda dheere dauda kar. Teri wajah se humari lag jati hai.*" [Run a bit more slowly. We're taken to task because of you.] He was the best. His house was filled with the gold medals he had won.'

After the drill, Shashidharan would compete in chin-ups and dips with the rest of the NCC members. The Renaissance man would not only motivate his fellows to maintain physical fitness, but would also encourage them to excel in academics. His friends remember how much inspiration they sought from him. He was particular about everything, even about the uniforms he wore. He would ensure that every button was in place and the creases rested at the right spots. That is how he was— excelling everywhere. Giving his best came naturally to this light-hearted jovial man, who believed nothing was impossible. No wonder his friends nicknamed him 'Tarzan'.

Major Kulkarni laughed genially when he said, 'You know Ma'am, Shashi's motto was, "Whatever I do, I will do with full *josh.*"'

He was a people's person, always surrounded by his friends. A kind and compassionate soul, he would be the first one to stand up and help a friend in need. His friends and seniors loved him dearly.

During the first year of college, he was recommended for the Technical Entry Scheme (TES) and had to report at the SSB, Allahabad. His financial condition was so bad that he did not even have money for the train reservation. All his NCC batchmates, juniors, and seniors, collected money for his travel and stay. Shashi was very hesitant about taking the money. It was against his nature to trouble anyone for his sake, but his friends told him how proud they were of his achievements. Shashi was recommended, but later rejected, over low position in the merit list. However, as expected, he was the first among the 2006 NCC batch to join the Academy through the CDS exam.

His mother, Lata Nair, had always been a significant influence in his life. He worshipped his mother. She had to work extra hours to ensure her children had the best she could afford. Shashi's friends remember how visiting Shashi's home meant they had to be there with empty stomachs because, no matter what, Aunty would ensure their plates were laden with piles of food she had cooked for them lovingly. Shashi was fond of spicy food. She cooked soya rice especially for him and his companions. It was also one of the most sought-after tiffin items during their breaks.

Major Kulkarni smiled from ear-to-ear when he mentioned an anecdote from their good old NCC days. 'None of us ever had money. We were broke. During our lunch break we would sit at our college canteen, open all the fifteen or twenty tiffin boxes together, and share our meals. We were a large group and occupied most of the canteen seats. Soon, the canteen owner realized that we sat there without paying a penny, and drove away his legitimate customers. He instructed us not to linger around if we did not order any food.

'Then onwards, the entire batch would be there for hours over an order of a single bun maska and chai. We were a genuine band of brothers; we would then share each other's tiffins. Shashi's soya rice was always a sought-after meal, and we would binge on it like people stuck in a famine. Those were lovely days. The bonhomie and warmth between us was unmatchable. The NCC values are very similar to those of the Army, where a brother-in-arms always occupies a corner of your heart.'

This was how Shashi had grown up—in an environment with little materialistic pleasure, but with exceptional human values. He had had a secure and happy childhood. Maybe it was just his upbringing in a modest Tamil Brahmin family. His parents did not have many resources, but they were generous and liberal. Practising the values of honesty and self-discipline, their family led a simple life that never had any place for inessential luxuries.

* * *

2006
Indian Military Academy

The tall and brawny boy dangled from a rope before jumping onto the thin wooden plank placed over a muddy ditch. Many kinds of obstacles made up the twenty-two hurdles a cadet is expected to cross on time. Gentleman Cadet Shashidharan V. Nair was the first among his peers to clear all of them in record time. His Ustads were proud. This cadet ran like an Olympic champion, which would always be an advantage to his Company, Basantar, for which he later won a record number of gold medals. He easily took the lead over the NDA cadets already trained and moulded. He was also an excellent basketball and football player, the games he had loved since his NCC days. Just like during his NCC days, now his IMA course mates complained, '*Thoda dheere dauda kar. Humari lag jati hai.* [Run slowly. We're screwed because of you.]'

Shashi would also take punishments enthusiastically. His back would be blood-soaked due to continuous rolling on bajaris and ragda on bare ground, but he never gave up on anything and did everything with full *josh*. Soon, he was a favourite with all his instructors and seniors. He was made Lance Corporal in his first term, and was appointed Junior Under Officer—a prestigious appointment—during the second term.

Shashi never forgot his NCC friends. He hardly got any time at the Academy but, whenever he got his privileges, he ensured he called them and guided them on the road to the Academy. Many of his course mates and juniors joined the Academy after him, and Shashi played a significant role in it as a guide, mentor, and role model.

During his time at the Academy, he developed a strong desire to join the glorious Gorkha Regiment. I remember, during a mess party, a Gorkha officer once said to me, 'Ma'am, one needs to be very fortunate to command the Gorkha troops, because it is where you command the utmost loyalty, devotion, and dedication from the finest lot of men.'

Shashi was indeed commissioned into the 2/1 Gorkha unit on 10 December 2007, after the completion of his IMA training. The 2/1 Gorkha Rifles, also known as the Veer Paltan, is one of the most decorated battalions of the Indian Army.

*　*　*

Pathankot
2009

Captain Shashidharan Vijay Nair had completed his mandatory commando training course and was back to his unit. He had also completed a Young Officer's course with instructional grading. The physical robustness, and his capabilities, soon made him the Company Commander of the Ghatak Platoon of his battalion. Only the best of the unit soldiers are included in a Ghatak Platoon, and Captain Shashidharan was among the best of the best to command them. It was not his physical prowess alone, but also his ability to mingle with the Gorkha troops, and his popularity among them, that pushed the Commanding Officer to appoint him to such a prominent position so early in his career.

Major Nair (then Captain) won the hearts of his troops during his 'line attachment', and his seniors could see it. Line attachment is an integral part of most infantry battalions, and the most important part of any Gorkha battalion where a newly commissioned officer is sent to live among the 'soldiers in line' for a month, to enable him to learn the language, culture, tradition, tasks, and emotions, of those he would soon command.

During this time, an officer performs every single task a soldier at the lowest rank is supposed to perform. It not only enables him to understand the technicalities and possibilities of a soldier's job at the lowest level, but also provides him with the confidence to command the men—considering he has completed the same tasks with excellence. During that time the officer is supposed to become 'one of many soldiers' first.

Captain Nair learned the Gurkhali language in no time. Soon, the Malayali boy from Maharashtra conversed with the troops in fluent Gurkhali. During *bara khana*, and on other occasions, he would dance the *Jhyaware* dances like crazy, putting his best foot forward, and sing songs in Gurkhali. It was difficult to imagine he was not born a Gorkha, but a Malayali, but then such are the qualities of a truly regimental officer.

While he was posted in Pathankot, he met Trupti in Pune in April 2009 for the first time through common friends. Captain Nair was shattered at that time, having lost his father to a heart attack. He was in Pune on a short leave to perform all the rites and rituals, but Destiny had its own plan. Some of Shashidharan and Trupti's common friends from Fergusson College were planning to meet over coffee at the popular college restaurant Savera—and they dragged both Shashi and Trupti with them.

It was love at first sight for Shashidharan. The shy girl, who hardly talked, stole his heart in an instant. Trupti was pursuing MCA from Fergusson College at that time, and was his junior. She was a Telugu, but spoke Marathi fluently. There were many similarities between them. Both south Indians had a family history of migration to Maharashtra, and both families had imbibed the Marathi culture heartily. But what amazed Shashidharan was Trupti's dancing skills. She was a trained dancer; she often performed in her college. She was quite popular too, and her dancing skills had their own fan-following.

The first meeting ignited a spark. She kept her distance, but the flamboyant Shashidharan did not give up on the girl who was the first one ever to knock at the door of his heart. He spent the rest of his leave hovering around Fergusson College, along with his old friends. Trupti soon noticed him and started mingling with them. It took time, but her interest was visible. Her innocence and shyness would astonish Captain Nair. His world was different from hers, despite their similar backgrounds. She was the stark opposite of Captain Nair's exuberant personality and, as their friends said, it was a case of 'opposites attract'.

* * *

January 2010
Pune

Trupti and Shashidharan had recently started conversing on mobile phones. The full recharge top-ups played Cupid between them. The ice was breaking; the shy girl had begun sharing her thoughts and feelings with him. Sometimes the night would turn into dawn in the blink of an eye. Beautiful poetry and Bollywood songs unfurled the romance in the air, and giggling over silly jokes would make up for all the miseries in the world. Captain Nair, the tough Ghatak Company Commander, would be on his knees before the shy young woman who danced like an angel and talked mostly through her eyes.

He was posted in Pathankot when he decided that enough was enough, and that now was the time to propose to her or be single forever. He was an excellent singer, one who could mimic Bollywood singers to perfection. His favourite song was 'Gulabi Aankhe Jo Teri Dekhin', but when it came to proposing to Trupti, he carefully chose 'Rehna Hai Tere Dil Mein', a song from the movie with the same title. They were conversing casually about the humdrum daily life, when he started singing the song and proposed to her by the end of it. Trupti was dumbfounded. She did not know how to react. She liked him for sure, but her increased heart rate did not allow her to say anything. She simply switched off her phone, leaving Shashidharan dangling on the rope of hope and despair the whole night.

That was the only time when the tough, brawny guy was scared—as Shashidharan later confessed to her. She, on the other hand, tossed and turned the whole night on her bed—with no trace of sleep in her eyes—trying to dig deeper into her heart. Shy girls are usually the most emotional, and so was Trupti. She never knew these feelings, but the morning brought clarity and she knew her answer. Before conveying it to Shashidharan, however, she went to a temple. She informed the Gods about her decision, and then decided to call him.

Captain Nair was in the office, trying to focus on his job. He looked dull to his CO, who asked him to take the day off, but Shashidharan did not want to go back to the loneliness of his bachelor's accommodation. It was then that the number he had been waiting for flashed on his mobile screen. He picked up his phone eagerly, and the first thing he heard was: 'YES!'

It took him a while to grasp the intensity of that 'YES!', but the next moment filled him with happiness he had never known existed in his heart. It was the start of a relationship that went beyond all logic and materialism, and pushed people to believe in love all over again.

* * *

June 2010
Pune

Captain Nair was on leave, but he kept it secret from Trupti. He loved giving surprises, unlike Trupti who hated it. Trupti had her semester break. One fine day, their common friend, Swati, called her and asked her to reach Savera for some urgent work. Trupti, with her sister Harsha, reached there immediately. When they met Swati, they found her happily placing orders. Right then Captain Nair walked in, and Trupti developed cold feet. She had never expected this. She ran outside in her nervousness. Harsha followed her out. 'What, Didi? Why did you run outside?' she said.

'I did not expect him here. I am not going inside,' Trupti replied.

Just like most sisters in the world, Harsha and Trupti were very close and shared everything. Though Harsha had never met Shashidharan, she knew all about him. She convinced Trupti to go inside and chat with the Captain. Swati and Harsha strolled outside casually, leaving the love birds alone. The coffee at Savera was a perfect choice, the buns tasted heavenly, and the smiles lingered longer. The couple decided to meet every day until Major Nair's leave ended.

That was the first of many days the lovebirds stole for themselves amid the cacophony of the world outside. Harsha would give a lift to Trupti under their mother Nilekha's nose, making excuses every day, and Captain Nair would hardly be home, leaving his mother Lata and sister Sheena bewildered over his unusual behaviour. The couple would roam around the whole city, painting it red.

Those days could be valued in gold for the two people madly in love. The power and intensity of those priceless moments could be felt only by Trupti and Shashi. The month-long leave flew by rather swiftly this time, and Captain Nair grew restless as the days to join the unit back again approached.

One day, early in the morning, he reached Trupti's house and stood right outside. He called her and asked her to meet him then and there. Trupti was perplexed. She had already lied to her mom too often. She knew her mother was traditional, and that she would never allow her to meet a boy under such circumstances. She decided to end the charade, went straight to her mother and said, 'Aai, my boyfriend has come and I have to go meet him.'

Nilekha was bewildered. 'What! You've been roaming around in your pyjamas since morning, and now you've suddenly acquired a boyfriend? Okay, call him here. Let me meet him as well.'

When Captain Nair met Trupti's mother, the first thing he said was, 'Namaste Aunty! I am Trupti's boyfriend.'

'Since when?' asked Nilekha.

The usually jovial Shashi was stiff with nervousnousness at meeting the mother of the love of his life. He said, 'Though we've known each other for the past year, it's just been six months of the relationship. But you see . . . it does not matter. We are going to marry each other.'

Nilekha tried to digest what he had told her. She said, 'Marriage? You decided already?'

Captain Shashidharan replied firmly, 'Yes. Whether anybody agrees to this or not, Trupti and I have decided to spend the rest of our lives together, and we don't see a future without each other.'

Nilekha said, 'Okay. We will see.'

Captain Nair returned to Pathankot, where he resumed his responsibilities. On 30 July, his birthday, he received a beautiful present from Trupti. It was a CD with a recording of 'My Heart Will Go On' from *Titanic*, in her own voice. She had recorded it in the bathroom of Harsha's office. She knew Shashi was fond of singing. He always encouraged her to sing, and had mentioned several times how they would sing duets during mess parties, after marriage. She had also bought a webcam, which was an expensive commodity those days, after saving every single penny she could, only for video calls with him. Since she stayed with her family, to sneak away right under the noses of her mother and brother was an arduous task for her, but she did it for love. Harsha had been a constant support for them. Nobody knew the little love story of the two bewildered hearts about to create a destiny that would soon inspire millions.

In December, Captain Nair returned to Pune on a month's leave, and this time he shared his feelings with his mother, and even took Trupti to his home to introduce them to each other.

Trupti told me the story during one of our conversations. She said, 'I brought a plant to gift to *Aai*. Shashi had once told me she was fond of plants, and I thought of gifting her one in a small planter. She looked very happy, and made me extremely comfortable. I won't lie; I was nervous, but soon her warmth paved the way for an everlasting relationship. She had laid a generous feast for me. I hardly eat, but that day I binged on it. As soon as she learnt about my dancing skills, she asked me to dance—and I danced like I was flying. Dance was my true calling. I always felt happy whenever I did it. She looked very impressed, and we chatted for a long time. Shashi mostly felt left out, but we did not pay much heed to him.'

I could feel the tinge of sadness in her voice. The girl who loved dancing would not even be able to walk one day. Cruel irony.

Soon Shashidharan visited Trupti's family with his mother and his siter, to fix the date of engagement. There was a little rift among the relatives because it would be an inter-caste and 'interstate' marriage. But the mothers took charge and they valued their children's happiness the most. Their engagement day was fixed as 11 May 2010. This time Shashidharan stayed with Trupti's family for a week, and left for Pathankot happily once his leave was over.

* * *

July 2010
Pathankot

Trupti and Captain Shashidharan Vijay Nair were engaged now. He wanted to introduce Trupti to his other family: the 2/1 Gorkha Rifles Gorkha Rifles unit officers and his paltan. He called Trupti to Pathankot on a short vacation. He introduced her to his friends and seniors, and took great pride in it. Trupti remembers how proudly he would mention her dancing skills before everyone. He would always say she danced like an angel. He also told everyone that he was going to get married on 12.12.2012. Shashidharan was not a superstitious man, but he was fascinated with this particular date. Throughout her trip, they did not stop chatting about their marriage and honeymoon plans. Those days are carefully wrapped, and shut away, in a box in her heart now. The memories turn painful when it's opened.

Within two months of her return from Pathankot, in October, Trupti started developing complications in her movements. She could feel the stress in her legs. The General Physician gave her Vitamin B Complex capsules. But it was only in November that her condition was diagnosed. Trupti had just attended her maternal uncle's wedding in Goa, and returned to Pune. The next morning brought sheer horror when, despite struggling hard, she found herself unable to move. Her vision had also blurred, and her eyeballs looked misshapen. A shriek escaped her mouth. Harsha and Nilekha rushed to her room and found her immobile on her bed, crying.

Trupti was shifted immediately to a nearby multispecialty hospital—Aditya Birla—where she was diagnosed with multiple sclerosis, a disease nobody had any idea about. The family started searching the Internet for information on this ailment. Those were desperate times. Her sister Harsha, brother Trilokesh, and mother Nilekha, also asked friends and relatives, and met all kinds of people in order to understand the problem and find a cure.

Trupti would keep crying. She suddenly lost the zeal to live. She was hopeless, sad, and shattered. Initially, nobody said anything to Captain Nair. They knew his unit had just moved to Gulmarg and his hands were full.

* * *

November 2010
Gulmarg
Kashmir

The unit had moved back to Gulmarg only a few months ago. The snow-capped mountains, huge poplar trees, and apple orchards, had replaced the austere simplicity of the plains. Behind the deceptive beauty lay regular bloodshed and violence. As a soldier, he knew his job was to curb terrorism and let Kashmir dwell on its beauty peacefully. The battalion soon took over the operational responsibilities at the new location. Captain Nair was appointed as a Company Commander at one of the high altitude posts, and was instrumental in the effective setting up of the Company in a counter infiltration role. He ensured the repair of existing infrastructure, and also added to it, so that his troops were comfortable. For him, the safety and security of his men mattered the most.

The areas along the Line of Control are prone to rampant infiltration by the terrorists, who use the natural cover of foliage, folds of the ground, and spells of inclement weather when the visibility is abysmal, thus necessitating the surveillance of every inch of the ground. The Company under Captain Nair created additional surveillance towers too. It was his vision.

Once summer had set in, and the snow had melted, Shashi was de-inducted to the Battalion HQs to perform the duties of Adjutant. At that point the battalion was also performing the duties of the security personnel of the Gulmarg bowl as the Bowl battalion. Gulmarg, known for its natural beauty, has snow slopes that attract a large number of foreign tourists who are primarily interested in skiing. Therefore, the security of the Gulmarg bowl was essential to ensure that the terrorists did not carry out any activities inimical to tourism in and around it. Captain Nair established an effective intelligence gathering team, incorporating the civil police administration that kept tabs on everybody (shop owners, tourist vehicle drivers, pony riders, hotel owners, etc).

He hardly had time to call home, but something disturbed him about Trupti's health. He could sense it, though everybody reassured him that everything was fine. Yet, there was something off about her. The chirpiness in her voice, and in their conversations, was gone. He waited eagerly for his December leave.

This time he did not go to his house in Khadakwasla, but straightaway reached Trupti's home. It was overwhelming for her and she started crying. For once the feeling of helplessness evaporated. She felt as if everything would be all right now that Shashi—her Shashi—was there. He went through all the medical reports and personally met the neurologist treating Trupti.

The neurologist said sympathetically, 'The maximum we can do is physiotherapy, because there is no treatment for Multiple Sclerosis. You have to understand that this disease has the potential to disable the brain and the central nervous system in many ways. This might result in the disruption of the usual activities of various body parts. The patient may experience physical or psychiatric problems. There could be double vision, or blurriness in the eyes, or even blindness. It could also result in the loss of coordination in parts of the body, and weakness in the muscles. However, I will try my best to manage her symptoms and also push for a speedy recovery.'

Captain Nair could not move for a second. It was disheartening. The doctor was talking about Trupti—his Trupti. But he was a battle-hardened soldier and, more than that, a great human being. In fact, he had never judged Trupti on her physical appearance, but it was her soul and spirit that he loved so dearly. He had seen his brothers-in-arms dying within seconds, or acquiring a disability due to enemy fire. He knew the essence of life, and how precious being alive itself was. By the time he reached Trupti's house again it was late in the evening, but the sun inside his heart was burning bright.

He asked Nilekha, Harsha, Trilokesh, and Trupti to gather in the drawing room, where he briefed them on the severity of Trupti's condition. Nilekha was in tears when she said to Shashidharan, 'Beta, I know it is tough, but you must break the engagement now. She may or may not walk again. It is in God's hands, but you must not ruin your life. It is a chronic disease. Trupti will always be a liability; you must carry on with your life.'

There was a stunned silence, broken only by Shashi's reply. '*Aai*, I cannot leave her. I love her soul, not her body. It's her spirit that matters to me, and I would certainly like her to keep that high. I am not going to leave her or break our engagement. Instead, I am thinking of getting married earlier—as soon as I get my next leave. Trupti is my responsibility, and I should be the one looking after her.'

Harsha intervened at this point, trying—she thought—to knock some sense into Shashi's head. She had always been a practical girl, unlike the emotional Trupti. She had played cupid in their story; she had watched their love blossom, but now she could not ask this man to marry her sister. But Shashidharan wouldn't listen. Trilokesh also asked him to be practical. Nilekha insisted again. After some time, Shashidharan lost his patience. He was firm and determined. He had always been the man in charge, and now was not the time he would allow someone else to decide his course of action.

He said politely but firmly, 'I request all of you not to intervene. It is between Trupti and me and, as I said on the first day, whether you agree or not we will be married. Please work upon marriage dates in April. I think I can get leave at that time.'

They surrendered, and so did Trupti. Shashi was her heart and soul. She poured every emotion she had ever known into their relationship. She did not know how to defy him because if there was anyone who understood her it was him. She also knew that in his place she would never have given up on him either. There are few relationships in life that push you to that extent against all odds. She knew theirs was one of those relationships.

Shashidharan spent the rest of his leave at Trupti's house, looking after her, supporting her, giving her courage, and more. When her hands shook, he would hold them; when her vision blurred, he would be her eyes; when her legs refused to move, he would carry her in his arms and take her to the washroom; and when she felt like crying, he would hug her tight.

Captain Nair uplifted everybody's morale, told them it was not the end, and it was okay to accept the situation and move forward with full *josh*. He would tell them stories about losing his friends; about hope, courage, and the destiny and miracles he had witnessed in his life. Eventually, he dragged Trupti out of depression. He would say, 'You cannot do anything about it. I know God has not been fair to you but, trust me, he could have been crueller. You have no control over your legs, but you certainly do over your will. Keep your spirit high, accept it, and move on.'

In between, he also met his family and informed them about Trupti's condition, uncertain of what was coming his way. He knew his mother was generous and kind, but he also knew how mothers loved their sons and dreamt of bringing home the best of daughters-in-law who would look after them during their old age. He was also aware that after his father's sudden demise, he was the sole breadwinner for his family. It was his responsibility to look after his mother and his sister too. He did not know how they would react to Trupti's condition, even though they liked her a lot.

His mother said, 'I am very proud of you, my son. If this had happened to my daughter, what then? Or what if Trupti had faced this condition after marriage? Could we have left her? No! I am pleased with your decision. She needs you more than us, and you must be with her all the time.' His sister Sheena listened to the conversation, nodding her approval.

That was an emotional moment. Shashidharan informed them about his decision to marry Trupti early, so that he could bear her medical expenses that came to around a lakh per month. The treatment of neurological diseases is among the costliest on the planet. He felt it was his responsibility rather than that of Trupti's family. His determination had doubled now that he had his family's support.

When Shashidharan rejoined his unit, he informed his Commanding Officer about his decision to get married soon—without mentioning Trutpi's condition. All his friends and colleagues I interviewed, mentioned how he never turned her problems into an issue or sought sympathy. From performing his duties, to going out or not going out for a party, Trupti's condition was never an excuse. For a long time they all knew she was a little sick, but that was all. For Captain Nair, she was normal.

* * *

April 2012
Pune

Once again Captain Nair was granted a month's leave, and he reached Pune ten days before his marriage on 24 April 2012. Just a day after his visit, Trupti had her second relapse. Her symptoms returned—the double vision, shaking, loose motions. She was immediately rushed to the hospital, and was admitted for several days for the administration of steroids. She was released on 19 April 2012, just four days before their wedding. Shashidharan did not leave her side even for a second.

During her interview Harsha told me the details. She said, '*Aai* and I finished all the shaadi shopping in one day. The guests had arrived, and the buzz suddenly turned happier at our place. We bought her a traditional Kerala Kasavu saree for the Malayali temple wedding in the morning—as Jiju was Malayali. Then we bought her a bridal Shalu Saree for the reception, typical of Marathi culture, which Trupti wanted. She was delighted to see her sarees and the bridal jewellery. Wedding festivities replaced the gloom in the air. All the relatives, now aware of Didi's medical condition, appreciated her choice of a life partner and admired Jiju a lot—even the ones who had initially opposed this marriage over inter-caste philosophies.' She sighed before she uttered the next words. 'On the wedding day Jiju and Didi both looked so happy and beautiful. I remember her smiling throughout the rituals. For the first time I saw her smiling since the tragedy had struck us.'

Trupti left with Shashidharan for their new home the day after marriage, where they spent some quality time with Lata and Sheena before leaving for Gulmarg together. The symptoms were in control, and Trupti could easily walk with a little support.

Trupti and Shashi spent some wonderful time together in Gulmarg. His leaves were over by that time. He had returned to his duties and would hardly be around her. The newlyweds stayed in the two-room fauji guestroom, and explored the scenic beauty of Kashmir whenever he was free.

The sweet shikhara and gondola rides, when Trupti would hold him tightly, are still etched in her mind. The summers had melted the snow a bit, but it was still freezing. The warm kahwa and the bonfires in the mess gardens are among her fondest memories today. At that time she felt as if together they had defeated the misery eager to clasp their happiness in its claws. She could see only love and marital bliss all around.

Strange are the ways in which this universe operates, working towards a future inspired by fortuity, supernatural forces, and actions in our past lives. Otherwise, wouldn't we be able to answer the question people like Trupti put to us: 'Why me?'

Trupti's condition deteriorated in Gulmarg. She had skipped some of her muscular injections, fearing high fever that enveloped her for two days each time she took them. The temperature had climbed so high that she needed special care but, since Shashi was always out on duty, she had decided to skip those. Whenever she took her injections, her condition worsened because of the cold climatic conditions. The unit was also about to shift to a new location. Advance parties had already started to move. She stayed there for two months before Shashi shifted her back to Pune—to her mother's place—to continue her medication and physiotherapy.

Trupti was admitted to Command Hospital in Pune. The muscular injections meant to control her symptoms had had an opposite effect. The doctors changed her medication, and put her on steroids, to be given intravenously every month. Soon, she had to be admitted to Command Hospital every month for four days, for her IV injection course, and later she would get back to her physiotherapy. Shashi boosted her morale.

He would say on the phone, '*Aab agali baar jab mai aaunga, to tu mujhe bilkul theek milni chahiye, bina sahare ke chalti hui.* [The next time I come, I should find you walking easily on your own.]'

The battalion was re-deployed at a different sector, and was now involved in active operations. The inhospitable terrain of the Shamshabari mountain ridge (generally the baseline for the LoC) Ridgeline was under the authority of Captain Nair and his Company. Once his Company was asked to surround a dense forest, where a terrorist group was likely to be hiding. They also had another battalion to support them. The operation started despite heavy rainfall, and everyone was drenched from top to bottom. The emergency ration the troops were carrying was over by day three, and they had to survive off the land, foraging for whatever was available. However, after seven days, with no successs, the operation was called off. Throughout the mission, Captain Nair displayed extreme courage and led his troops from the front. He could not call Trupti at that time and, when he did, she cried for hours. Shashi was her whole world.

Trupti tried her best. She worked hard on herself. She aspired to get better for the beautiful life she dreamt of with Shashi. It was only a matter of time. Meanwhile, the unit moved to Gandhinagar, and Shashi decided to bring her down from Pune. They could start their married life properly. Once he was settled, he took Trupti with him, though it was difficult for both of them. Every month Shashidharan would drive her to Pune for her IV injections, because they were not available in Gandhinagar. They would start in the evening and reach Pune early in the morning, and immediately admit Trupti to Command Hospital. He would stay with her for the next four days, after which they would quickly drive back to Gandhinagar. It was their monthly ritual for the next year and a half.

Captain Nair was a dedicated son, brother, and husband, but first he was a dedicated soldier. His duty came first and foremost, and then his wife. His personal life never affected his professional competence, and he continued to excel there.

The unit was in peace, and families were allowed to stay together. Trupti had established her first proper home and Captain Nair had also picked up his next rank in 2013. She had kept a maid, who would do the cutting and chopping for her, and Trupti did the rest of the cooking all by herself. Though Major Nair urged her not to work in the kitchen, she knew what a foodie he was and loved cooking for him herself. She used a walker to walk.

Many officers mentioned how Major Nair carried Trupti to the mess in his arms so that she would not miss any bit of fauji life. He would carry her in his arms even for a picnic or an outing. He loved taking her everywhere he was invited. She was never a liability for him, but always his better half. Life was good. Later, he asked for a posting to Pune on compassionate grounds for Trupti's treatment, and was posted to the College of Military Engineering (CME), Pune, as an instructor.

They got a large house in Kirkee. Trupti decorated every corner of that place. She knew how social Shashi was, and how he loved throwing parties for everyone. On weekends their family members from either side would arrive, and they would party all night. Often Trupti stumbled while walking from one room to another and was put on a wheelchair. Though she used it, she never felt confined to it. She fondly remembers her time in Pune.

She said, 'Shashi loved travelling and exploring things. There must not be any restaurant or pub in Pune where he did not take me. Many times we would go with family and friends. He did not like me to stay back alone, and made sure I attended all his mess parties. It also helped me learn a lot about the Army culture. At times we invited all the unit officers at our place, and cocktails went on till the wee hours of the morning.'

'Almost every weekend Harsha and *Aai* came to stay with us. Shashi looked super excited those days as *Aai* would cook many non-vegetarian delicacies for him. Sheena and Shashi's mother also visited us frequently. We would go out, eat out, shop, and do much more.' There was a brief pause before she said, 'Those days seem unreal now.'

And when everything felt as if it was falling into its place, Trupti was detected with Human Polyomavirus 2. It was the side effect of the IV injections she had been taking. The virus had lowered her immunity, weakened her body's internal defences, and infected the blood. She was instantly taken off the IV injections and given tablets instead. Her physiotherapy was improved.

But the couple never lost hope. Shashidharan still kept her morale high. Life was meant to be lived to the fullest. By 2016, the 2/1 Gorkha had moved to the field location in the Nowshera sector, and Major Nair's tenure in Pune was also supposed to be over. He had a few competitive courses to complete, and he was eagerly waiting to rejoin his unit. He knew how every single soldier in the unit counted at a location near the LoC.

Meanwhile, Harsha married a Kashmiri colleague and shifted into her husband's flat. Nilekha would thank her deities for the happiness all around. She felt fortunate to have such wonderful sons-in-law, who were no less than sons to her. But happiness is fragile. One moment you feel you have it under control, and the very next it might slip away. The world moves at its own pace, has its share of sadness and happiness, and its own way of saying to us mortals, 'You are not God'.

* * *

May 2017
Lam, Nowshera

The peaceful Valley of Lam at the Indian side of the LoC was suddenly in a tense situation after the Uri attack on 18 September 2016. The intense provocations led India to carry out surgical strikes, and the conflict at the LoC flared up. The Pakistani Army violated ceasefire several times a day, and resorted to heavy firing and mortar shelling to target several Indian forward posts and civilian areas. Lam was one such forward post.[5] Bullets rained the whole day. There was continuous shelling of mortar bombs, Rocket-propelled grenades, and firing from heavy machine guns (HMGs), along with smaller arms from the enemy.

The surgical strike in 2016 was a blow to the enemy's morale, but they retaliated aggressively. Even after India declared that it wouldn't carry out other surgical strikes, the Pakistani military was insecure about its terror launch pads in Pakistan-occupied-Kashmir (PoK). It was where they regularly recruited and trained young men to become terrorists and infiltrate India across the LoC. These launch pads were the target of India's surgical strike. Platoons of the regular Pakistani Army were deployed to safeguard them. The increased and insane artillery shelling was a part of their plot to rattle the Indian side. They also increased the infiltration squads to enter the Indian terrority.

The Pakistani masterminds planned to infiltrate the Indian borders in large numbers to avenge the surgical strike. The infiltration attempts would be assisted by the Pakistani posts. The Pakistani Army also pushed the local terrorists to cause damage to the Indian Army. They would plant IEDs in large numbers, targeting the patrolling parties.

The constant provocation pushed the Indian Army to retaliate. The situation at Lam changed overnight. The Valley was not prepared for a war-like situation. In such tense circumstances, Major Nair rejoined the unit in May, and took charge as the Alpha Company Commander. There were times when the shells reached the unit langar. Heavy causalities were reported; several soldiers, including officers, lost their lives or were injured. The Commanding Officer faced the challenge to stop the causalities and retaliate effectively. Company Commanders would be on their toes. The Junior Commisioned Officers (JCOs) would come to them and say 'Saheb, *aise to humari poori Company saaf ho jayegi.* [Saheb, our entire Company will be wiped out like this.]'

The frequency of Indian patrols in the area, and the number of ambushes, increased manyfold. BAT actions (by the Pakistani Border Action Team) and blasts were a daily occurrence, along with cross firing and terrorist activity.

One of the officers, Lt Col Dev Anand, who was at 2IC (the second senior most in the unit) of the 2/1 Gorkha

Rifles at that time, said, 'Lam, otherwise a peaceful terrain, suddenly turned out to be a very dangerous area to operate in. Any step could be the last step the moment we crossed our defences. We all would pray silently to God for taking care of us, and bringing the men back safely. Not that we were afraid but, as soldiers, you don't want to die in vain. Dying along with a few enemies is always the aim.'

Company Commanders started preparing a good defensive operation. The bunkers were erected, fences strengthened, and mines laid. At the LoC you don't require any informant network. It is a frontal war: artillery shelling and a spray of bullets from across the borders. Infiltration of foreign terrorists is a matter of concern. The patrol parties would frequently guard their areas, and the Company Commanders themselves would perform night duties alongside the jawans. The Pakistani side would continue with provocative ceasefire violations, and the Indian troops would retaliate effectively.

But the bigger challenge was to stop the infiltration. A larger number of terrorists tried to infiltrate the borders every day—assisted by the Pakistani posts. The Indian Army carried out extensive patrols for area domination. The brave Indian Army soldiers performed their duties despite being aware of the constant risk to their lives amidst heightened tension. Technical surveillance, drone deployment, and the use of illuminators, were also increased by the 2/1 Gorkha Rifles deployed close to the LoC.

Major Shashidharan Vijay Nair and his Company retaliated against cross-border firing with full vengeance. He killed many members of the Pakistani BAT and the terrorists. Once during the patrols, as his Company foiled the infiltration bids, an intense firefight ensued between them. It eventually forced the foreign terrorists to return to PoK. It was a daring act by Major Nair and his Company under the heavy shelling. The intense firefight, so close to the LoC, to push back the militants was also a risky task. It was a straight giveaway regarding their locations, to the Pakisatni Rangers nearby. But it was typical of Major Nair's daredevilry his colleagues remember him for.

'He had a daredevil attitude. He never believed in failure or defeat. He would take the initiative, and try and try until he registered a victory. He was a true Gorkha soldier who believed in Naam, Namak, and *Nishan* more than anything else,' said the Major's then Commanding Officer, Col Lalit Jain.

Major Nair's presence was a big morale booster for his Company and the unit. The Commanding Officer trusted his decisions with complete confidence. Many competitive courses were waiting to be completed by him. They were essential for his rise in the Army, but he was reluctant to leave his unit at such a difficult time. This speaks highly of his commitment.

He met Trupti in April 2018 for a short time, when she was shifting to her mother's house from their fauji accommodation. He promised her he would take leave in July for his cousin's wedding. In June, however, one of the 2/1 Gorkha officers lost a leg in an IED blast. There was a severe shortage of officers, and asking for leave at that time felt unethical to him. He had imbibed the OLQs officer-like qualities (OLQs) too well. He knew how emotional

Trupti was, so he hardly ever mentioned his problems or circumstances to her, but he said, 'My unit needs me more, Trupti. Animesh Sir has lost his leg. Even if I come, I'll only be able to bring my heart to you, but I'll be leaving my mind here'.

* * *

7 August 2018
Pune

Trupti was watching television when the news about Major Kaustubh Rane from the 36 RR battalion deployed in the Gurez sector in Jammu and Kashmir flashed.[6] He had attained martyrdom during counter-insurgency operations. This news hit Trupti with an intensity she had never expected. She almost lost control. She knew Shashi was also operating in a nearby area in Kashmir, and situations were always risky even when he gave his family his standard answer: '*Arrey*, what will happen to me? Everything is fine. *Yahaan to bas aish hi aish. Maze kar raha hun.* [It's party time here. I'm enjoying myself.]'

Nilekha had asked Trupti to cook rajma. She entered the room right at that moment to find her pouring water on the floor instead of over the rajma. The floor was all wet, and Trupti cried continuously. Nilekha turned around and took in the TV newsflash. She switched it off hurriedly and hugged her daughter. Trupti went on crying. She said, 'I keep telling Shashi to come back quickly. He does not even go for his courses. It is very risky there. I pray for it to get over, so that he comes back soon. *Aai*, please pray he comes back soon.'

Trupti kept waiting for his leave, without realizing how tense the situation at the border was. It would be a long time before his next visit to her, when he would wipe her tears, broaden her smile, and bring back the sparkle in her eyes. Whenever he called, he said, '*Main jab tak aaunga, tu mujhe chalti hui milni chaiye, koi bahana nahi.* [By the time I visit, you must start walking. No excuses.]' And Trupti would try harder—for him. She dreamt of the days when she would be walking and managing everything on her own, just like regular couples did.

Hope lingered in Trupti's heart amidst the despair of having Shashi at one of the most dangerous places on earth. This is the story of most Army wives, who are pretty used to swinging between hope and despair, love and loss. Trupti was no exception, except that she could not walk, and the support she sought was far away serving the nation with pride and dignity. All she could do was wait and pray.

* * *

August 2018
Somewhere at the Line of Control

The 2/1 Gorkha battalion had been successful in preparing a good defensive operation, resulting in fewer casualties. The troops had also settled in, and the unit retaliated every time the Pakistanis violated ceasefire. The trading of bullets would sometimes last the whole day. It was taxing, challenging, and risky. The increasing infiltration proved to be a headache for the battalion. Major Animesh had been saved from the IED blast, but was now leading the life of a disabled man.

Major Nair was outraged at the incident, and wanted to stop others once and for all. He informed his Commanding officer, Col Lalit Jain, that he was going for a patrol into his area. He went to the far end of the Indian side of the LoC, very close to the Pakistani posts. It was a life-threatening situation. All it would have taken was one peek, and a bullet would have shot him down. He was very well aware of it, but he still took the risk for the sake of complete enemy posts profiling. He wanted to know the minutest of details that the enemy was trying to hide from them, and he was determined to crack their code. His Quick Response Team (QRT) was waiting for him at some distance. It was his commitment to his men that whenever he sensed a life-threatening situation, he put himself forward and asked his men to follow behind.

When he came back, he had much information regarding the enemy posts. En route he had also surveyed a few tentative areas that could have served as secure infiltration gateways. This daring stunt helped his unit plan and execute many operations in the future. Next, Major Nair established mines in the area, including the one near the LoC. Again, it was a risky operation, yet he came back victorious without a scratch on him or his men. He was relieved after securing the area. Who knows how many of his brothers would have lost their lives otherwise?

He didn't know he was soon going to lose his own in a rather unfortunate incident only a few months later.

* * *

December 2018
Pune
Nilekha's residence, Kirkee

'Hello.' The happy voice echoed once Trupti picked up the phone. It was the voice she craved and waited for, for days.

'Hi, Shashi! How come you called me at noon? I am flattered. I have stopped sleeping, so that I don't miss your calls at unearthly hours,' Trupti replied in Marathi.

'*Arrey, tu ye sab chor. Ye bata tu kar kya rahi hai?* [Forget that. Tell me, what have you been up to?]'

'Nobody is home. I am watching TV.'

Usually, Nilekha locked the front door of the house during daytime when she went out. They had two maids, who would check on Trupti once in a while till she returned.

'If you are alone, who will give you food, Trupti?'

'Sutar Maushi will come at 2.00 p.m. and serve it to me.'

'*Arrey*, but the door is usually locked. How will she enter?'

'*Arrey Baba*, the keys are in the planter outside. She picks them up and comes in,' said Trupti.

She swears it must have been only a moment later that she found the tall and very handsome Shashi standing right before her. He loved giving surprises, and it had been a long time since he had met her. Recently, he had had a strange urge to see her as soon as possible. Some new officers had recently joined the unit, and he had quickly applied for a month's leave. He had called her standing right at the door. It overwhelmed her. The loneliness vanished within seconds. She could smell only love and joy in the air. Her soulmate—her Shashi—was back. She held him tight and cried for a long time.

It was as if he wanted to make up for the lost time—with the family—with a vengeance. Unlike other times he ensured that he met all his friends and relatives. He even went to Chandigarh to meet his cousin, who had been asking him to visit for ages. He could not go to Khadakwasla this time, to his mother's place, because the roads leading to his house were damaged. It would have been impossible to carry Trupti along. So he asked Lata and Sheena to visit them at Kirkee. Then he made a plan for a visit to the Andamans. One of his closest friends and brother officers, Major Prasad Tithe, was posted there, and he had asked Shashi to visit him with Trupti. Tithe knew he went nowhere without her.

Trupti said, 'Out of the blue Shashi booked our tickets with my brother. I was neither well, nor inclined to go, but he insisted. He said, "*Tu chal ab. Ye last trip hai; iske baad pata nahi hoga ki nahi. Main bahut* busy *hone wala hun.*[Just come. This will be the last trip. After this I'm going to be very busy.]" I still wonder why he said so, because it was indeed our last trip together.'

It was a beautiful trip. Shashi, Trupti, Tithe, and his wife, would sit near the beach, close to their fauji accommodation where waves of laughter would flow, and jokes would never stop. Major Tithe remembers how Trupti complained that Shashi had not made any investments, and they needed to save for the future through some policies, while Shashidharan laughed it off saying, 'Why take any policies when nothing about life is permanent?'

When they came back—even though it had been a beautiful trip—Trupti said she felt uneasy all the time. Shashi was to leave on 1 January 2019. For the first time she asked him to stay on and leave only after Makar Sankranti on 14 January. But he did not stay. The last thing he said before catching his 5.00 a.m. flight was: '*Agar ruk sakta to ruk jata, Trupti. Rukna* possible *hi nahi hai.* [I would have stayed if I could, but it's just not possible.]'

* * *

11 January 2019
Nowshera sector
10.00 a.m.

Major Nair was distraught. He had just received a call regarding the critical injuries of the twenty-four-year-old Rifleman Jiwan Gurung from his Company. Rifleman Gurung in the Reconnaissance and Surveillance team was supposed to go on leave from 12 January 2019. Only days earlier he had interviewed the young, ever-smiling boy from Darjeeling—and presented him before the Commanding Officer for further briefing. Major Nair took it upon himself to avenge the boy. He held a powerful sense of ownership and devotion towards his unit and the boys he commanded. He was enraged about the IED blasts in the morning that had caused injuries to his men.

He called the Commanding Officer Colonel Lalit Jain. 'Jai Hind, Sir!'

The CO sensed something was not right, since Major Nair had called him at this time. 'Jai Hind, Shashi. Tell me, what happened?'

'Sir, I have a piece of bad news for you. Rifleman Jiwan Gurung is critically injured.'

The CO could feel his heart sinking. He had lost many brothers over his long and illustrious career, but such news always hit the mind and soul with the same intensity.

'Jiwan Gurung? The boy I interviewed yesterday? He was very excited about meeting his family again. It's been months since he met his mother. How did this happen?'

'He was out on a regular patrol on a recce-and-surveillance mission, when their vehicle met an IED blast. He was in the co-driver's seat. The rest of our men are injured, but not critical.'

'Okay. Let me inform the Commander and I will get back to you. I will reach the spot soon.' Col Jain didn't know that not only would they lose Rifleman Gurung, who would succumb to his injuries soon, but that this would also be his last conversation with Major Shashidharan Vijay Nair, the gem of his unit.

In fact, Major Nair never came to know about Rifleman Jiwan Gurung succumbing to his injuries later. He immortalized himself in an IED blast only a few hours later.

The moment Major Nair hung up, he received a message from his sister Sheena, who informed him that their mother had fallen sick. Her blood pressure was very high, and she was taking her to the hospital. He asked to her to keep him posted as he left for the blast site along with his QRT.

Major Nair knew his Commanding Officer would soon visit the site. He needed to carry out a combing operation to secure the area against any other IEDs, as a standard procedure. There was a high risk of more IEDs around the area after the first blast, and there could also be threats from the terrorists hidden in the area. He could task his QRT with the job, or wait for the bomb disposal squad to arrive, but his regiment always took centre stage when it came to making a decision. He knew the bomb disposal squad would take time, and he was not in the mood for any more casualties.

* * *

Col Lalit Jain, after informing his senior, left for the blast site with his QRT. Major Nair, on the other hand, started sanitizing the area, keeping himself in front of their formation. The Company Commanders are critical for the mission's success, and also responsible for the overall morale of the Company. However, unlike in the standard formation, where the Company Commanders usually walk behind scouts, Major Nair decided to walk as the first man (scout who has the maximum probability coming in line of danger in case of threat).

He was aware of the danger, and he decided to risk his own life rather than that of any of his men. They were going down the slope towards the blast site, when he saw a wrecked jeep and debris scattered all around. From a distance, he also saw Col Jain reaching the spot from the opposite side. He had also started surveying the area with his team. Their QRTs from either side of the blast site would occasionally fire at the surrounding bushes to flush out hiding terrorists looking for an opportunity to cause more damage.

Major Nair suddenly sensed something amiss at the spot in front him. They were around twenty metres from the blast site, approximately forty metres away from the CO's party. He suddenly ordered his QRT of ten people to halt. He said he would move alone first, and that they should move if he signalled. His JCO tried to dissuade him, and requested to be allowed to accompany him, but Major Nair was adamant. He asked him to follow his orders and wait till the coast was clear. He checked his WhatsApp messages, and found a message from Sheena saying that their mother was well. More tests had to be done the next day. They were returning home. He heaved a sigh of relief and moved forward, towards oblivion.

The other QRT team was looking for the camera Rifleman Gurung had been carrying with him, when they heard a loud blast. They dived down to cover themselves, thinking they had been attacked. It only took them a moment to realize that the explosion had occurred towards Major Nair's side. They could not cross over immediately because the area between them was not yet sanitized, and moving forward meant risking more lives. They took out their super-zoom cameras and binoculars to take a look.

That was when the troops standing helplessly on the other side, at some distance, signalled to indicate the supreme sacrifice made by Major Nair.

There was gloom in the air. Col Lalit Jain could feel the sadness engulf his body and soul. Later he said to me, 'His mortal remains were just some thirty-odd metres from me, but I felt helpless like I had never felt before. I could not move forward to extricate them, for the sake of other precious lives. I could not jeopardize the safety of more men under my command. I had lost Gurung and Shashi both in one day. A sense of loss, so strong, crawled over me. I wanted to run to the blast site, but I could not since it wasn't sanitized. Various emotions churned within me as I wasn't able to do anything. Eventually, I called the Commander and requested a bomb squad for a fresh combing operation. Those were the most disappointing and excruciating moments of my life—waiting until the engineering team arrived.'

* * *

11 January 2019
Pune

Trupti's brother, Trilokesh, received the call from the unit and was the first one to hear the devastating news. He informed everyone except Trupti. No one had either the courage or the heart to tell her. Unit officers, along with their wives, started visiting her house, and the air turned melancholic with each arriving visitor. The teary-eyed and grief-stricken faces were enough for Trupti to sense that her fears had come true. She was numb. It felt as if a black hole had sucked her inside. Nothing mattered after that.

Trilokesh called Sheena and informed her he was coming to visit her with one of Major Nair's unit officers. Sheena thought her brother must have told them about her mother's health and they must be coming to meet *Aai*. Though it was dark and late, she happily replied they could visit any time. Her mother had just gone to sleep. She thought she would wake her up after they arrived. It was the fear of waking her up that had not allowed the TV lover to switch the TV on that day, when every news channel was playing the news about the 'veergati' of her brother.

She kept waiting but, when they did not arrive by 10.00 p.m., she called Trilokesh and asked him to visit the next day. However, he insisted on coming right then, and asked her to leave the door open beforehand. Something had happened. Sheena said to me, 'I don't know why, but suddenly dark and dismal feelings surrounded me. At once my instincts told me something was wrong with Bhaiya. Even though Bhabi used to be sick, never once did it occurr to me that something could happen to her. I rushed to Mamma's room to check on her; she was sleeping. I locked the door quietly and came out of the house. My best friend appeared and hugged me. She was crying. Trilokesh and the unit officer had also arrived by then. People started pouring in, and the phone would not stop ringing.' She said she should have cried, but something held her back. Her protective feelings towards her mother strengthened her resolve to keep the news from her as long as she could. She requested all the mourners to return in the morning once her mother's medical tests were done. Lata had high BP, and giving her the news in such circumstances would have been risky.

In the morning she cooked breakfast for her mother. She knew her mother wouldn't be able to eat from then on. Then she took her to the hospital. The damaged road, not repaired in decades in front of their house, had miraculously been repaired overnight. Herds of people were gathering around and tents were being erected. Her mother murmured something, but Sheena did not reply. Once all the tests were done, Sheena went to her mother and told her about Major Nair. Then, they cried—theirs were the tears of the forsaken.

A little later Lata hugged her daughter tightly, and said, 'Don't cry, Sheena, your brother has embraced death as a hero. You should be proud of him. We all have to die some day, but how many people get the opportunity to die for the nation? Don't mourn his death; don't cry here. It is a hospital. Everybody here is already troubled. Don't cause them more pain.'

Friends and family had reached the hospital by then, and they were stunned to see the courage of the mother of the soldier who had just made the supreme sacrifice. Theirs was the bloodline of heroes—like mother, like son.

* * *

12 January 2019
Pune

The Junior Commissioned Officer, who brought back the mortal remains of Major Shashidharan Vijay Nair, folded his hands before Lata, and said with tears in his eyes, '*Aapke bete ne hum sabko bacha liya. Agar* Saheb *nahi hote to hum sab maare jaate.* [Your son saved our lives. Had Saheb not been there, all of us would have died.]' Those were the tears of gratitude for an officer who preferred sacrificing his own life to his men's on the battlefield.

When Lata met Trupti, she held her tight. Trupti was numb. She stared into the void without reacting to anything. Even Nilekha, Trilokesh, and Harsha were inconsolable. The loss was too big. Lata and Sheena took charge of the situation. Harsha told me the details later. She said, 'I have seen mothers panicking over the scratches their children get, but Lata Aunty stood like a pillar for all of us. She consoled not only Trupti but all of us. It was only because of her that we could try to overcome the grief and pull ourselves together in the dreadful situation.'

The funeral on 13 January was suitable to a hero's stature but, for Trupti, life lost all charm after the incident. Lata was the one who pulled her out of the excruciating pain. She said, 'Trupti, you have to understand Shashi was not just a common man, but a hero. He died like a hero. He is now a feeling for all of us. We cannot take him out of our memories, but we certainly need to learn to live without him. We must do everything he wanted us to do. Do you remember how he always wanted you to walk, do your work by yourself, and start a business? I believe you can do all of that. Try harder; don't give up. For him—for Shashi.'

I had heard angels roam among us, but it was when I heard Lata Aunty's story that I believed it. I also wondered at the existence of a mother-in-law like her in a society where some other in-laws often burn their daughters-in-law for dowry. Not only the family members, but also all the officers in Major Nair's unit vouch for her grace, dignity, and courage. Col Jain, Major Nair's then Commanding Officer, told me he visited them to console them, but it was Lata Aunty who comforted him instead. She was proud of being a warrior's mother, and proud of his sacrifices. The pride in her heart for her son matches the pride 2/1 Gorkha battlion holds in his sacrifice.

You will be astonished to know about another woman of the substance in this story, Mrs Nita Ambani. She willingly agreed to bear Trupti's monthly expenses for medication— around Rs 50,000—when a veteran Gorkha officer, Major Gen. Kumar, and then the 2IC Lt Col Dev Anand, approached her for financial help. The Reliance Foundation readily agreed to reimburse the cost of physiotherapy and employed a full-time nurse for Trupti for the next five years. The support was personally approved by Mrs Ambani, who was touched by the story Major Nair and his wife. Coming from a private organization, it was a huge gesture, and she made it away from the eyes of the media.

All the ladies and officers of the Gorkha unit came forward to help Trupti collectively. It was the cohesiveness and the spirit of the Gorkha family, which provided her support and gave her strength to sail through the tough times. Today, Trupti works from home as an HR manager for a private firm, Midasblue, and claims that her boss, Bhairavi Kamat, is the best boss ever. Her wounds are still fresh. It was challenging for her to speak up when I approached her for the book. Initially she declined but, after some days, she called me back herself and said that she would tell me the story and relive those moments through my book. She also said, 'I am trying hard to move ahead with life and to keep pace with it. I am also working harder on my physiotherapy. It is for the legacy of the bravest man I ever knew. I will not give up on life.'

Trupti still struggles with her health, and lives with her mother, while Lata and Sheena keep visiting her. Lata continues with her tuitions, and Sheena has recently taken up a job. Recently, Trupti visited Shashi's unit and his Company, which gave her immense satisfaction. Though she doesn't find much to look forward to in her life, she is taking one step at a time to move ahead. Tears still fill her eyes at the mention of Shashi's name.

* * *

The story is based on the interviews with Major Shashidharan Nair's wife Trupti,[7] sister Sheena, sister-in-law Harsha, brother officers Lt Col Milind Kulkarni, and Lt Col Thithe. Major Nair's then Commanding Officer Col Lalit Jain, and the 2IC Lt Col Dev Anand, readily agreed to this interview to honour the memories of their comrade-in-arms.

Never Give Up

Major Priya Semwal and
Naik Amit Sharma

Haridwar
24 June 2012

A crushed and grieving Priya sat at an awkward angle, jammed into a small corner of the room. She was forcing herself to face the people around. There was an ocean of them. It was the funeral of a soldier killed in action after all. And many of his companions regarded him with feeling, almost religious devotion. Naik Amit Sharma, the lad who had been killed in action, was the pride of the family. A few children ran around, but Priya could not see her five-year-old daughter—Khwaish. She did not bother to locate her either. Her world, as she had known it, had just collapsed.

The atmosphere was mournful. Female relatives were howling and tearing their hair. There was also deep silence during mealtime in the house of mourning. Nothing mattered now, not even her existence. It was confusing.

She wanted to lie down and mourn in silence, away from all the people, but it was not possible. She had to sit there and be tagged as a 'bechari'. Her mother reached out to embrace her. She didn't know whether to console her or to cry on her shoulder herself. Priya looked at her wrinkled face. Her mother had begun to look several years older within a span of a few days.

The voices grew in intensity; the incessant whispers swung between viciousness and apathy:

'*Ma-beti dono widhwa hai. Kya naseeb leke aayi hai bechari.* [Mother and daughter both are widows. What horrible destiny.]'

'*Paise kisko milne hain? Biwi ko ya ladke ki ma ko?* [Who will get the money? The wife or the boy's mother?]'

'*Widhwa ho gayi bechari, ab kya karegi paison ka?* [The poor woman is a widow now. What will she do with the money?]'

'*Bhari jawani me widhwa, baap bhi nahi hai. Beti bhi hai. Bhagwan na dikhaye aise din kisi jo. Bechari.* [She's been widowed so young. She has no father to turn to either. An she has a little daughter besides. Nobody should have such a fate. Poor woman.]'

'*Iski ma ko dekh, kya karegi aab? Natini bhi itni choti hai.* [Look at her mother. What will she do now? Her granddaughter too is so young.]'

She swallowed every remark and rubbed her hands in her lap—desperately. Her eyes were bloodshot; she looked as tired as she felt—dishevelled hair and dark circles beneath her blazing black eyes. She had not just lost her husband—the one she loved with all her heart—but her existence as well. It was a brutal realization that left her devastated, and pushed her from hope to despair within thirteen days.

The 'Terahvin' marks the end of the mourning period which lasts thirteen days from the day of the cremation of the deceased. Those thirteen days are meant for the rituals performed for the sake of salvation of the departed soul. These thirteen days provided a lot of time to Priya to mourn. She felt alone and depressed, and even howled at nights remembering Amit—who had promised to walk beside her for the next seven lives.

Priya knew this was not salvation. Shattered, she would lie down on the bed and stare at the flame in the lantern. Sometimes she looked in the mirror, scrubbed her face vigorously, panicked, and wondered in utter dismay—why her? Sometimes she would wake up panting in her damp sari, from the nightmares of her dead husband. But what troubled her the most was the consistent taunts from the people that shrunk her dignity. People forgot she was not just a widow, but a flesh-and-blood person. Suddenly, not only her own identity but the identities of her mother and her daughter were also forgotten. They were not persons any more, but rather a bunch of weak, meaningless women, not eligible for a respectable social status.

The women did not see a grieving young woman, rather a widow, a 'bechari' who had almost lost the right to live as a free citizen. Priya lived in a society surrounded by endless myths and stigmas. She certainly did not belong to the progressive class, but came from a conservative background where women lived in shackles and under limitations. Her resources were also limited, and so was her financial condition.

Cruel remarks thrown casually at her made her life miserable, and the mourning almost intolerable. There was also a point when she felt she was losing the will to live, but her beautiful five-year-old daughter, Khwaish, whom the couple had named with hope and happiness when she was born three years after their marriage, on 16 July 2007, helped her cope. It was as if all their wishes had been fulfilled with her arrival, and their life was complete.

Priya's mother was utterly devastated. She had lost her husband two years ago due to cardiac arrest. Now she had her widowed daughter dealing with the same fate right before her eyes. She knew how brutal the world could be to widowed women, and she was scared for her daughter. She could bear everything, but her daughter, her young daughter . . . She was inconsolable! She remembered the time when she had asked Priya to get married.

* * *

2005
Jakhan Rajpur Road
Dehradun

Priya had just finished her class-twelve boards, and taken admission in BSc first year at DAV PG College, Dehradun. She was only nineteen. Mrs Vishakha Semwal had been offered a nice 'rishta' for her only daughter by a close friend; the prospective groom was a soldier in the Indian Army. Uttarakhand is a land of warriors. At least one person from every family seems to serve in the Indian Army. Vishakha was happy that a proposal had come all by itself. Soon the boy's family visited their house, and she liked the boy a lot.

The boy, Amit Sharma, was well mannered and suave. He wore a crisp ironed shirt and polished shoes. He looked very serious, and said, 'I am looking not only for a wife, but also a life partner. You don't need to worry about her education. We will not stop her from pursuing her studies. She will study as much as she wants.'

Priya found the boy enchanting. His tales from far-off lands where he had served, and his anecdotes from his training days, would make her smile. Amit also fell for the girl who believed in independence, and valued her education. Being a soldier he knew he had found his better half, who would never bow down to the circumstances in his absence. His soldierly instincts sensed the soldier in Priya. He loved her spark.

They soon had a huge Garhwali marriage ceremony, which hundreds of folks from several neighbouring villages attended. After marriage Priya shifted to her new house, a few kilometres away from her mother's place. Those initial days just after their wedding were like a dream come true. Amit opened up to her about his job, which she knew nothing about, but she was proud to have married a soldier. She realized how considerate and affectionate he was. He would bother about the slightest things that mattered to her, and try his best to fulfil her wishes. He would also encourage her to study more when he himself was just a 'twelfth-passed'.

They would also often go on long bike trips, eat Maggie, drink tea in the cold fog typical of Uttarakhand weather. They were meant to be together—perfectly complementing each other—where one was incomplete without the other. Soon, with promises to come back quickly to his new bride, Amit left to rejoin his unit.

Those days were all sunshine and rainbow, sweetness and light. Priya continued her studies and attended classes at DAV College. The days were spent waiting for Amit's call—and that one call at unearthly hours would make up for everything. She wouldn't stop talking, and Amit heard her without getting tired.

Priya Semwal, who was a little girl only sometime ago, started taking on responsibilities in her life. She would help her mother-in-law in the kitchen, cook, clean, and study. Sometimes she would also visit her mother after her college hours. Amit would call her almost every day, share the tidbits from his life, and she would listen carefully. Before putting the phone down, there was one thing Amit never forgot: to remind her to study well and study more. She was happy in her life and, when Amit returned on leave, he would wrap her in all his love.

Amit would be eager to visit his in-laws, and visited them as soon as possible. Touching their feet never sufficed. He would hug his-mother-in law fondly, demanding all sort of delicacies, while mocking Priya for her cooking skills. Vishaka could not stop smiling over their sweet little fights.

When I met Vishakha Semwal, Priya Semwal's mother, the woman epitomized grace. Her smile warmed up the little drawing-room of Priya's fauji accommodation. Priya was out for her evening PT—Then a Captain. The tastefully done drawing-room walls showcased framed pictures from the OTA. The OTA bell, engraved with the OTA song 'Roshni'—*Bharat ke Hum Jawan, Parvat ke Hain Samaan*—hung carelessly at one corner. There was a picture of Priya with her daughter, Khawaish, and right beside it were several framed medals won by Priya. She had won gold and silver medals in various sports and competitions back at the OTA. The rest of the room was occupied by Military Engineer Services (MES) furniture.

Aunty met me affectionately, and told me how Amit had loved her food. Once her anecdotes about Naik Sharma were finished, both of us cried over the man who had meant so much to the Semwal family, and the terrible separation of the two people who were supposed to grow old together. Theirs was the story of love, loss, longing, and courage.

'Beta, he loved whatever I cooked, and he would put his demands forward every time he visited us. He would come to the kitchen, sit on the slab, crack jokes, and ask me to cook his favourite dishes. Never for a second did I feel he was our son-in-law; rather he was a son.' Her eyes were moist, remembering the good times. 'He stood rock solid beside us when we lost Priya's father to a heart attack. Priya was inconsolable, and I was shattered. My son, Pravesh, also lost his zeal. Amit stood by us, and helped us cope with the grief. But even before we could stop mourning the death of Priya's father, Amit too was gone. The tragedy of our life feels surreal—as if the grief is an illusion, and nothing like this can really happen to anybody. However, this is a reality. Only God knows how much strength it has taken us to reach where we are today. You know, Beta, you can never get over the loss of someone who gave you a reason to smile.' She choked over her words.

I hated my job. There is nothing worse than watching a mother cry. I hated the cause of it in my heart. I did not know what to do at that moment, or how to console Aunty. I was sorry about reminding her of the greatest loss she had had, and I was sorry to talk about it. But the reason—i.e., bringing out these stories to hundreds of grieving women like her, to tell them they were not alone, and to tell people about these extraordinary women who have lost everything for this nation—stayed at the bottom of my heart. I cried with her. I did not know how to console her, so I left quietly. It was raining outside, but it did not matter.

When you meet Major Priya Semwal, she will blow your mind with her confidence and fortitude. An undaunted woman in olive green. The bright young EME officer (from the Corps of Electronic and Mechanical Engineers) commands respect from hundreds of soldiers today and symbolizes OLQs. It is unbelievable that she has faced such personal tragedies. The boldness she displays is unimaginable. She could not let hopelessness or devastation seize her.

* * *

There were times when nothing except Amit mattered in Priya's life. The newly wedded couple cared about each other and were more of friends than lovers. Naik Amit

Sharma was not loaded with either time or money. He had a humble source of income from his government job, and he was allowed around two months of leave in a year, but it was never a hindrance for the devotion he had for Priya.

Sometimes Priya fell sick, and he spent money like water, providing her with the best of everything. He also refused to leave her side when she was admitted to the hospital due to her health complications. At times he would hold her hands for hours, listening to her never-ending stories. Sometimes he made tea for her, and even did her college projects. This kind of sensitivity penetrated Priya's mind and offered her satisfaction. These memories helped her sail through the rough patches whenever she felt alone or abandoned later in life.

The date 16 July 2007 was perhaps the happiest for Amit and Priya—when Khwaish was born. Priya said, 'Amit was elated beyond belief. His face lit up as if he had got his favourite toy. He would talk about how Khwaish would be educated in a convent school, how he would put every luxury of this world at her feet, and how I had made him the happiest man on the planet. When I look back today, I feel—when you have a partner who cares so deeply about you, provides you with every comfort, does not try to cage you, enables you to conquer the world, and tries to make you happy with his every move—you feel only love. But once that support is snatched away, the effects can be devastating as well as life-altering. The same thing happened to me.'

* * *

25 May 2012
Dehradun

The brand new four-wheeler was delivered on Amit's birthday at their residence. Amit's leave was about to end, and he booked his return ticket for 30 May 2012. Nobody knew it was his last visit to his loved ones. As if he had a premonition, he ensured that he met each one of his long lost friends and relatives. The four-wheeler was actually for his darling wife. He refused to take the keys, and said to the Maruti representative, 'Please present the keys to Madam. She is the rightful owner of this car.'

Priya blushed. She insisted that Amit should drive the car first, while he said she should be the one to do it first. He wanted her to be completely independent. He learnt to drive the car in two days, and promised to take Priya to Chamba Valley in their new vehicle the next time he came home. Little did she know that such a time would never come, and those moments spent with Amit were soon going to turn into precious memories.

* * *

20 June 2012
Arunachal Pradesh

Senior JCO Baldev Singh from the 14 Rajput, Amit's unit, called Priya Semwal at around 9.00 p.m. and asked her for her in-laws' number. She suddenly started palpitating. Though the JCO pretended to be casual, and reassured her about Amit's well-being, somehow she knew something was not right. Amit had reached a transit camp on 17 June, and informed her about his move to a forward post soon— from where communication wouldn't be possible. He had also said something disturbing on the 19th when she asked him why he had not gone to the forward post yet. He said, '*Accha hai, yaar, jitney din neeche rah lo. Upar to bus pareshani hai. Fir tumse baat bhi nahi ho payegi. Ye hume taqleef deta hai.* [It's better this way, man. The longer you stay down here the better. Up there you only find trouble. Besides, we won't be able to talk. That thought gives me pain.]'

Amit was a true soldier, and it was not the first time that he was getting deployed in such an area. She still wonders why he said so.

The senior JCO hung up once she said she would ask her in-laws to give him a call. But Priya could feel her stomach churning. Her heart beat apprehensively, unable to process things objectively. She asked her elder brother to give the JCO a call, pretending to be her father-in-law. Once he called the man in question, he was informed that Amit had been killed in Operation Orchid once his convoy plunged into a deep gorge. The vehicle had fallen while taking a turn at a steep mountain. The fauji routes on the North-eastern hilly terrains, especially at the forward posts in Arunanchal Pradesh, were indeed dangerous owing to unconstructed roads, terrible weather, and hazardous tracks. Descending into the steep valley always involved risks the soldiers took voluntarily.

The pictures of the mangled remains of the convoy vehicle at the bottom of the gorge, kept carefully in the war diary of the 14 Rajput, still do not allow Priya to sleep. There were sixteen people in that convoy. All of them had miraculously escaped death, sustaining minor injuries, except for Amit—who had sustained massive head injuries which killed him on the spot.

Life was never the same after that. Once she had been everything, and now she was 'just a widow'. When she wanted to mourn, the society around her did not let her. They asked her cruel questions, tagged her with the word she hated the most—bechari. Once the terahvin ceremonies were completed, and people headed back to their homes, Priya's mother insisted that Priya should come and stay with her, but she did not. She was scared of facing the neighbourhood she had grown up in, where people knew her well. After Amit was gone, staying at her in-laws' place, where every other thing reminded her of him, was equally painful.

Eventually, her brother counselled her and took her back to their home at Jhakan Rajput. There would always be people, neighbours, and relatives who wanted to meet her, but she was not ready to hear another word reminding her of her status. Fortunately, her mother understood her. She never revealed to her neighbours that Priya lived with them now, and allowed her to mourn in peace. Priya suffered every day.

With great losses comes great suffering; with great suffering comes great strength; and with great strength come life-altering decisions. Sometimes, when you feel all roads are blocked, God suddenly shows you the path to a new destination. One day, Priya received a call from the Commanding Officer, 14 Rajput, Col Arun Aggarwal. He said, 'Hello. Priya Beta, I am your husband's Commanding officer. I called to offer you condolences, and to let you know that Amit was one of the finest we had.'

All he could hear on the other side of the phone were little sobs. He himself was grieving. He was a true regimental officer, who had promised himself when he took over his command, that no matter what he would ensure the complete safety of his men. Amit was the first casualty of the 14 Rajput during his tenure. Col Aggarwal held a deep sense of responsibility towards Amit and his family. He further said, 'Priya, Amit mentioned how educated you are, and he was extremely proud of the fact. If you truly want to pay tribute to him, appear for the SSB exam. Use your education for greater good.'

The statement was received with deep silence on the other side of the phone. Then Priya replied, 'CO Saheb, I am sorry but I don't have any courage left. Life is meaningless. Thank you for calling. Namaste.'

It was their first conversation. Col Aggarwal understood her state of mind, and knew it would take time to heal, but he desperately wanted to support her. He pursued Priya's brother, Pravesh, and convinced him. Pravesh counselled Priya about the SSB exam and the empowerment it would bring her. Pravesh had been a Defence aspirant himself once.

Priya Semwal started thinking of the SSB exam. She felt the society would not let her live with dignity otherwise. She would always have to live with the status quo. That was not acceptable to her. In those dark days, with the help of her brother and Col Arun Aggarwal, she understood that there was only one way to win her dignity back—by cracking the SSB exam. It was also the only way for her to take the legacy of her husband forward, and provide a respectable status to her mother and her daughter. For Priya Semwal it was already a battle for pride.

She then discussed the process of cracking the SSB exam in detail with the then Commanding Officer. He promised to help in every possible manner. With complete support from the 14 Rajput, Priya filled the SSB exam forms in Meerut. Then she returned to Dehradun and started preparing for it. She would wake up at dawn, so that no one could see her doing the physical exercises. Her elder brother stood like a rock beside her. He had attempted the same exam many times, and he turned out to be a natural mentor and guide to his sister. He said to her, 'In the SSB exam the panel comprises highly qualified officers. They know it all, so never for a second think you can fool them. Just be who you are, just show what you are. Don't say yes to the things you think you would be incapable of. Never lie in your SSB exam.'

He would run beside his sister early in the morning, and they would return home once the first sunlight reached the earth. This also helped Priya to focus on a goal, and fight against her depression. She was so occupied with her aim that her pain subsided.

* * *

22 November 2012
Allahabad

Priya wrote an account of her own life when she was given a blank paper to write a story during the SSB psychological test. She completed the obstacle course in two-and-a-half minutes instead of three minutes, despite high fever. When asked during the interview about her decision to join the Army, she said, 'I don't want to join the Army for name, fame, money, or luxury, but to honour the legacy of my husband and to restore dignity to my mother and my daughter.'

She was recommended, but now her medical examination on 27 November would be the deciding factor. And on that basis she was rejected. The medical officer went through her kidney reports, which said she had once been operated for kidney stones. Though the civil doctors had cleared her, somehow that particular medical officer declared her unfit.

Her brother, Pravesh, cried before him. 'Sir, this is for the first time that a Jawan's wife has come so far. Because of one decision of yours she won't be able to achieve an extraordinary feat. Please don't do this.'

The medical officer would not listen. He said, 'I am just following the rules. Please try next year.'

Every tear Pravesh shed pierced Priya's heart. If there was anything she was left with, it was only her pride, and she saw it getting tossed away mercilessly. She held her brother's hand and dragged him out of the doctor's room.

Once outside she called the Commanding Officer, Arun Aggarwal, whose support and encouragement were the reason she had appeared for the SSB exam in the first place. She was crying. From the other side of the STD phone he said, 'Never give up! How many times do I need to tell you never to give up, Priya? You have made it so far. I am sure you will make it. You are a brave woman. You have faced things you were not supposed to face; this is nothing. You know, when I told people about your selection, everybody laughed at me. They said an OR's wife could not be an officer. You have to prove them wrong. Go back to the guest room and meet the Commandant tomorrow morning. Tell him about yourself.'

He was indeed right about people taking Priya casually. Never before had a jawan's wife donned the uniform. It was indeed an impossible feat that Priya turned into a reality through sheer grit and determination.[8]

While speaking to me, Priya said, 'I came from a background where nobody either knew anything about the fauj or bothered about it. Even I did not know anything. Had it not been for Col Arun Aggarwal, I would have never made it. The 14 Rajput Regiment supported me at every step like a family—from my guestroom arrangements, to commute, to everything else.'

Next morning both the siblings reached the Commandant's office at around 6.00 a.m., but they were called inside at 3.00 p.m. They were exhausted by then. Hope did not allow them to move from the visitor's room even for eating or drinking but, when they met him, he said since the reports had already been produced he could not help Priya with anything. This was heartbreaking, but what pushed Priya beyond the limits of human tolerance was when the Commandant offered her a job as his PA. Her outburst shook him.

She said, 'I am not standing before you for a job. I have an MSc in Mathematics; I have a BEd degree. I have cleared the CTET, and every other teacher-eligibility test out there. If I want employment, I will get it any time. This is not about employment. Rather it is about pride and dignity. I want to carry forward the legacy of my husband, who lost his life for the nation. Hope you understand this.'

The Commandant was taken aback by the raw courage and confidence of the timid girl, who didn't look even sixteen. He then asked her to make a last appeal at the Research and Referral Hospital, New Delhi.

During our conversation her lips twitched, and wrinkles appeared on her forehead when she said, 'Ma'am, I am glad I learnt these hard lessons early in my life. When you are nobody, no one bothers about you. You are nothing but a speck of insignificance in people's eyes, and they derive pleasure from humiliating you. But I am thankful to such people and such remarks that turned me into the person I am today. They made me braver, more passionate, and dedicated to my goal. So we went back to Dehradun, heartbroken, but not broken, and decided to do the kidney tests again.'

She was eventually cleared by the medical board at R&R, New Delhi, and all the Generals and Brigadiers in the panel congratulated her wholeheartedly. The Chairman, a Maj. Gen. ranked officer, said, 'It is a great achievement. I hope many more follow in your footsteps. I wish you all the very best. You have made us all very proud. God bless you, Beta.'

* * *

13 April 2013
OTA, Chennai

As soon as Priya stepped into the Academy, her hair was chopped off for the classic crew cut, along with sixty-three other Lady Cadets and 300 Gentlemen Cadets, who joined the OTA, Chennai. The Lady Cadets were divided into two Companies, Zojila and Phillora. Do you remember the intense inter-house rivalries in the Harry Potter stories, where the houses are just not houses but the identities of the students for which they fight fiercely? The same goes for the Companies in military academies. The Companies participate in various inter-company events competitively, and maintain proper decorum and discipline to win the coveted banner at the end of the term. It is a matter of do-or-die for the Companies.

In Indian Military Academies, you stop existing as an individual; cadets aim to foster the feeling of camaraderie and better relations with their peers. The right conduct and high merit of a cadet impact the whole Company, and a lousy performance brings a series of severe punishments. In the times to come Lady Cadet (LC) Priya Semwal was going to take Zojila Company to new heights.

Major Sushmita Gaur, Major Priya Semwal's course mate, said to me, 'Frankly, we all thought Priya would take advantage of her status as a war widow. She was offered several privileges, such as an accommodation inside the Academy to allow her to live with her daughter, relaxed training, etcetera. We all knew it had only been a few months since her husband passed away, and she was grieving. But, to our dismay, she rejected assistance, including the accommodation in the premises to live with her daughter, and requested the authorities to treat her like any other cadet. Initially, she had to struggle a lot with her communication skills and other things, but watching her I learnt that winners never give up. She earned the prestigious appointment as a Corporal in the junior term soon.

'You know Semwal's best quality? She was a tremendous leader, and she kept the whole Company together. Being the Corporal she underwent punishments, sometimes even on behalf of others, but she accepted them enthusiastically. There were times when *bajari* was put inside her T-shirt, and she was asked to roll on the ground. She ended up bleeding profusely. But she would finish the drill spiritedly. Eventually all our seniors, Directing Staff (DS), and saab log ended up praising her, and pushed our limits citing her courage and performance. It was as if the word "no" never existed in her dictionary.'

The OTA days were unlike anything Priya had experienced before. Everything was challenging, but she was determined to prove that she deserved to wear the uniform because she had earned it through her blood, toil, and sweat, and not because of mercy.

The days would start early—at 5.30 a.m.—and basically never end. The gruelling physical training exercises, academic studies, punishments, sports, and competitions, hardly left time even to sleep. The cadets perpetually lived in a state of sleep deprivation.

Priya smiles every time she remembers her training days. When I asked her to provide me with an anecdote from the OTA days, she laughingly shared an incident about how a Lady Cadet was once found missing during weapon training.

'The firing range was outside the OTA,' she said. 'Once we reached the place, I started counting and found a Lady Cadet missing. I was the Corporal, and it was the Corporal's duty to ensure everybody's presence. When JCO Saab found out about it, he said I was good for nothing, and he would ensure my Company got the strictest of punishments. He also asked me to roll over the stones, while he ordered the rest of the Company to find her. They all started searching for her frantically. Then Saab received a call from MT (Military Transport) that a Lady Cadet had returned sleeping on the bus. (Cadets in military academies are so sleep-deprived, they can sleep anywhere any time). She was sent to the firing range again and, once she reached, the whole Company was made to roll on the ground. After the firing practice, when we returned to our barracks, we found our seniors waiting for us with another set of punishments which continued for several days.' She laughed so much that tears appeared in her eyes. 'Oh, I miss those days.'

She went on to describe how the regular days would start with 'muster fall-in' or early morning roll call, followed by the morning parade comprising PT and drill, after which all the cadets would rush back to their Companies, shower, change, have their breakfast, and rush again to attend their first class—all within half an hour, which was an impossible task, considering the Company location, dormitories, drill square, the mess, and the classrooms, were separated from each other by at least two or three kilometres.

'Ma'am, that harrowing schedule taught us a lot about life, especially how time management is everything,' said Priya.

I could see her eyes shining with pride. She mentioned how the DS would always check for military bearing and discipline. The campus was filled with figures of authority. Officers, JCOs, Ustads, or seniors, roamed the campus with prying eyes for random offences by cadets—such as over speeding while riding the bike, single mounting (not moving around on the bike with a squad), improper turnout, improper saluting, wiping sweat during the drill, and many similar offences, which would invite a series of punishments.

But that was not the end. The late hours of the night brought forth another facet of the training, where the senior Lady Cadets made sure to teach them some lessons in humility and discipline by giving them more punishments. Those punishments were given over the slightest of mistakes. They would order the juniors to perform various rigorous egg rolls, back rolls, front rolls, side rolls, cream rolls, bajari order, brick order, murga patti, maharaja, helicopter, whiskey, star jumps, and other exercises. These fancy names involved manoeuvring the body at all possible angles while rolling on rugged ground, standing on one foot, performing a headstand, and other torturous activities that would easily be categorized as third degree if the police inflicted them. But they also made for memories of a lifetime for the cadets. After the punishment, just before dawn, they would start preparing for yet another day at the Academy. The wee hours of the morning were also the time to finish their assignments and projects.

I have heard millions of Academy stories from my husband, and many other Army officers just like Priya Semwal, and they have all made me believe that even Usain Bolt, the world's fastest man, cannot match the speed at which the poor cadets perform their daily duties. No wonder our soldiers are the best in the world. The pressure tactics back at the Academies turn them into men and women of steel physically and mentally. They learn that nothing is impossible. By the end of the term Priya, and two other Lady Cadets, were the only ones to clear ATP (All Test Pass) at their first attempt.

* * *

June 2013
Dehradun

Priya had taken three days' special leave to attend her late husband's *barsi*. Her daughter flinched when she tried to hug her, because she could not recognize her. Priya had short hair and her complexion had darkened, her palms had blisters, and her personality had changed. Relatives, who had gathered to pay homage to her husband, murmured:

> '*Ladka lag rahi hai puri. Mard hai mard.* [She looks like a man. She's turned into a male.]'
>
> '*Pati ko mare ek saal bhi nahi hua, baal kata liye. Bahut hi giri hui aurat hai.* [It hasn't even been a year since her

husband died, and she's chopped off her hair. What a
fallen woman.]'

All kinds of taunts were thrown her way, but the woman
of substance, and the face of true woman empowerment,
LC Priya Semwal did not flinch. To me she said, 'I knew
my husband was proud of me, wherever he was. You focus
on negativity only when you want to disturb your rhythm.
When you have a goal, and you focus on it with a laser
beam, you develop a mental blockade against negativity.
I knew I had a higher purpose in life.'

She won the gold medal in a highly competitive
and prestigious cross-country race once she was back at
the OTA. She had a fever, yet she ran beautifully. Her
Company was very proud of her, and so was the Adjutant
on the horse who ran with the first cadet who ran ahead of
everybody else in a cross-country race. The Adjutant was
Lt Col Naveen D. Prabhu from the 14 Rajput Regiment—
her husband's unit. It was a matter of personal pride for
him that Priya belonged to the 14 Rajput family. It was
because of her that Zojila Company won the cross-country
race.

Remembering old times she told me gleefully how
she and LC Sushmita Gaur, her best friend, were caught
sleeping in an ATM booth by a senior. Exhaustion, sleep
deprivation, and the Chennai heat, had tempted them to
sneak inside that ATM because of its air conditioning, but
they were eventually caught and punished severely. Now
that she had men working under her directions, those days
felt like another lifetime.

When I asked Major Sushmita about it, she laughed happily. The warm vibes of the golden days perhaps reminded the responsible officer of the mischiefs they got up to as young cadets. She also narrated another incident about how both the Companies were asked to make surveillance towers, and the rival Phillora Company went on making theirs aggressively even after their twenty-four-hour time period was over. Zojila Company was perplexed, and they kept asking Priya, their Corporal, for instructions. Priya said to them calmly, 'Let Phillora do it first, and then we will do it.' She started constructing the tower an hour before the inspection, and they won the competition.

Sushmita said, 'I know you won't believe me, but she was the best of us all. She would take the initiative in every task, and pave the way for the rest of the Company. It was always teamwork for her. She acted like a true leader. For instance, when we went on camping exercises, she would dig the soil, settle things down, and then we charged forward.'

After giggling over their adventures as young cadets, and listing Major Priya Semwal's achievements with utmost pride, Major Sushmita also told me that inside the tough-looking Semwal hid an emotional woman—one who cried the whole night when she could not attend her brother Pravesh's wedding. Both the siblings were extremely close, and Pravesh had stood with her through thick and thin. Attending his marriage was a dream Priya had dreamt for years, but she could not make it due to the training. Had she requested the senior authorities, she might have been granted a day's leave as a special privilege to a war widow, but that was against her ethics. She did not ask. She called her brother at 2.00 a.m. that day, once she was free, and cried the rest of the night holding Sushmita tight.

* * *

September 2013
OTA Chennai

Lady Cadet Priya Semwal was now in the second term. Her fitness had improved, and so had her performance. She had earned her well deserved Coy Sergeant Major (CSM) appointment in the senior term on her merit. This time Priya ran the cross-country race of nine kilometres instead of six as she had in the first term. Her course mates came to her and said, '*Tere chakkar me humari bus bajti rahti hai. Thoda slow daudiyo.* [All of us get into trouble because of you. Run a little slower.]' During their cross-country race, Priya ran so fast that she was not even visible. Unaware of that, the Phillora Company Ustads were thrilled, and taunted the Zojila Ustads that the Phillora Lady Cadet was winning the race this time against Zojila Company's fastest runner, Priya Semwal. Precisely at that moment one of Zojila Company's Ustads pointed out that Priya Semwal was already standing at the finishing line. Priya won the gold medal in record time, and Zojila won the prestigious race. For a long time the Zojila Company Ustads kept reminding their rival Ustads of this win.

During Priya's Battle Proficiency Efficiency Test (BPET), where hundreds of Gentleman Cadets (GCs) ran with the Lady Cadets (LCs), the drill Ustads placed bets that Semwal would beat the Gentlemen Cadets. True to her reputation, she ran beside the GCs and won. It hampered the GCs' morale severely. Their Ustads were offended and kept shouting, '*Doob maro saalon! Ek Lady Cadet tumse se accha daudti hai. Uska pace dekho. Sharam karo.* [Go jump into a well, you fools! A woman can run faster than you. Look at her pace. Shame on you.]'

The pressure mounted, and all the Gentlemen Cadets ended up giving their best. The criteria for judging the male and female cadets were different. All the GCs thought they must have failed the BPET since an LC had defeated them. They were completely unaware that LC Semwal had run so fast that the Gentlemen Cadets were in the 'excellent' time slot because they had tried to keep pace with her. Later they thanked her, and said that her fearlessness had inspired them to push their limits.

By the end of the second term she was enjoying a reputation very few cadets did. Nobody ever remembered she was a war widow. The haplessness of being a widow had vanished under her achievements.

There was no pressure to appear sombre, no limitations or constraints imposed upon her for being a vulnerable war widow. Every Sunday she would make two calls: one to her daughter, Khawiash, and the other to Col Arun Aggarwal. Priya hailed from a humble background where nobody understood her situation. Officers like Col Aggarwal were an asset to the organization, who genuinely bothered about their men and their families. He would guide her, console her when she was upset, and tell her never to give up when she was about to break, only because he had promised himself, over the dead body of Naik Amit Sharma in the morgue, that he would always look after his family.

Sometimes Priya and Sushmita would sit silently together. Those moments were important. They knew words would simply dilute the tranquillity; instead their solitude defined their friendship. Sometimes Priya would miss her husband and grieve over his untimely departure, and at other times she would miss her daughter. There would be regrets and guilt at staying away from little Khwaish. She would say to Sushmita, 'I know it is not fair to Khwaish. I abandoned her when she needed me the most. She has no father, no mother, and she misses us both, but one day she will be proud of me and understand why I did what I had to do. I want to raise her like an Army brat with dignity—and I will do it.'

The time to take the Antim Pag, and wear those golden stars, was approaching. The drills and the physical training had been made more intense. The prestigious 'march and shoot' competition, which held the utmost importance for passing out of the Academy, was also approaching. For the competition cadets were asked to run two-and-a-half kilometres, cross obstacles, climb the rope, cross a six-metre long wall, and then, crawling through difficult trenches filled with mud carrying a heavy rifle, fire. Cadets could not afford to fail it. Priya excelled in that competition.

On the day of the passing-out parade she performed the sword drill—a highly prestigious movement only the crème de la crème performed—and also won the coveted

Half Blue certificate and the Best Lady Cadet award. She had two merit cards for cross-country, and gold medals in various sports. Col Aggarwal, her mother, her brother, and her daughter were present for the event, and their proud smiles made her realize that everything had been worth chasing. More Gentlemen Cadets came to her and made a confession. They said, '*Jab tu daudati thi humare saath, to humein lagta tha ki hum slow daud rahe hain, par humein humesa baad me pata chalta tha ki hum excellent mein hain.* [Whenever you ran with us, we always felt we were slow runners. Only later did we realize that we actually fell in the "excellent" category.]'

The Lady Cadets threw her in the air once, circled her, and said, 'Thank you, Semwal. It was because of you that we were motivated to push our boundaries. We began to think that if you could make it with your child, and your emotional turmoil, why couldn't we? You pushed us to give our best.'

When our interview was about to finish, the undaunted woman gave me a typical fauji smile, adjusted her pee cap and said, 'I am proud of my training. I have achieved what I wanted. I have broken barriers against all odds, because I wanted to prove that women are not a weaker gender. I hope my story will inspire women all across the country to have faith in their capabilities. The OTA has trained me well, and now I am no more a "bechari" for anyone. Never give up.'

The stars on her shoulders shone; the creaseless uniform added aura to her personality, and her confidence intimidated the soldiers standing in front of her to take orders for their next assignment. I wished her luck and moved out of her office with great pride in my heart. I now knew not just an empowered woman, but also an incredible one.

* * *

The story is based on interviews with Mrs Vishakha Semwal, mother of Priya Semwal; Col Arun Aggarwal, the then Commanding Officer of the 14 Rajput; Major Sushmita Gaur, Major Priya Semwal's course mate; and Major Priya Semwal. She had picked up rank by the time the book was published. She achieved a feat almost impossible at that time. Today we see many war widows joining the Forces, and very few of them come from an NCO background, but back in 2012 it was unheard of. It was only because of the Commanding Officer, the 14 Rajput, who believed in progressive ideas and encouragement, that a Jawan's wife could join the Forces. Today many Commanding Officers of the Indian Army are following in his footsteps and investing their efforts in enabling war widows to achieve something in their lives, which is a great societal change in the recent times. Now Priya commands respect from thousands of men serving under her. Her daughter lives with her. The grief she hides is invisible, until you dig deep and reach those emotions that make her a woman just like any of us.

The Last Gift

Sujata and Major Satish Dahiya, Shaurya Chakra (P)

10 February 2011
Pawera
Haryana

Sujata looked like an angel in her pink sari. The glowing bride-to-be wore traditional Haryanvi bridal jewellery: a cartilage ear clip in the shape of a *karanphool*, a *ranihaar*, and a *chhaj* that sat daintily on her forehead, covering half of her face. When she walked down the aisle, people gasped. She could not stop glowing on her engagement day.

She giggled with her friends and cousins, who teased her for getting engaged to an Army officer unexpectedly, when all her life she had maintained she would not marry early. Her parents and family were thrilled. The venue for the function at her village in Pawera was jam-packed. People from several villages had come for a glimpse of the groom. Captain Satish Dahiya from Banihari Village was the only Army officer in the surrounding area. He was basking in the glory of being a Haryanvi groom.

Sujata and her family had not seen the groom yet. It was only during the engagement ceremony that she could steal a glance at him. She was not impressed. Satish looked rough and tough. His round face was tanned and carried several bruises. Though he looked confident, he was undoubtedly not physically attractive. She had always hoped her life partner to be clean-shaven and sleek.

When Ritu, her friend, nudged her, and said, '*Aur bata?* Do you like him? Blushing already?'

Sujata replied, 'I don't know . . . He—kind of—looks arrogant. He has not made any attempt to interact with me yet. And who gets engaged so early in the morning? What is wrong with the boy's side?'

'The boy's father, Sri Achal Singh Dahiya ji is an ardent devotee of a Pandit ji,' said Ritu. 'He said 7.00 a.m. was the most auspicious time.'

They both giggled together. Sujata stole a glance at Satish and her eyes met his. He stared too. Immediately, she looked away. That was the only interaction Sujata had with Satish that day.

Theirs was an arranged marriage. Common relatives had seen them on behalf of each other, and proposed a match. Satish's parents were in a great rush, and asked the girl's side to have the engagement in March 2011—when he was expected to come home on leave. Satish arrived in February, earlier than expected, and the girl's side had to rush for arrangements at short notice.

It had been two years since he was commissioned as an Army Service Corps (ASC) officer. He could only spend about a month and a half with his parents during that time. He was attached to the 1 Naga Regiment based at Nowgam, Jammu and Kashmir. It was his first posting. His parents had tried to hook him up with several girls, but it was only Sujata's picture that caught his eye. His parents were afraid he would change his mind, and insisted on a quick marriage.

Sujata, the small-town shy girl whose world was limited to her home and college, was unaware of the world to which Satish belonged. She had no idea about how forward posts in Kashmir could take a toll on the Indian Army soldiers and change them completely. The high-altitude postings could be unforgiving even for the toughest. Frequent blizzards and sub-zero temperatures created the most hostile environment to live in, let alone fight. Hypoxia, debilitating frostbite; cold, cruel ultraviolet radiations, and giant avalanches were a daily reality. Sometimes a brother-in-arms could slip and fall towards the enemy side, or simply die of High Altitude Pulmonary Edema (HAPE).

The terrorists also had a habit of intruding at unearthly hours, but a soldier took everything on his chin as a part of his life. He shed no tears and continued doing his duty to the best of his ability, battling the odds and the enemy, in such incredibly difficult conditions.

Once back from such postings, soldiers needed time to readjust to, and keep pace with, life in the city. Satish had been hugely tanned as a consequence of being in the snow at an active Indian Army post in Kashmir. The life back with the Naga Regiment was different. Months would go by when he would not even shave. His physical appearance, body mass, and even psyche were not regular. The engagement, too, could not take place as planned and had to be advanced. During a recent counter-insurgency operation, he had injured his back, and was exempted from active duties for a while. The Commanding Office asked him to go on an early leave and get done with the wedding ceremony rather than wait till March.

All the unit officers, including the Commanding Officer, were aware of his engagement. They were the first ones to see Sujata's picture sent by Satish's parents. The Second-in-command (2IC) of the unit was the first person to receive the photograph. He opened it and wrote 'approved' at the back of the picture. Then that picture rotated among the whole unit, before reaching Captain Satish Dahiya at a forward post. The back of the image was filled with the comment 'approved' by the other unit officers. Satish was excited. He, too, liked the girl and said yes to his parents. However, between his injury and the engagement, he did not get any time for personal grooming and reached the ceremony as he was.

The ceremony went off very well, except that the boy and girl could not interact. The next day Satish called Sujata several times, but she could not take the call before evening.

'*Agar aapko hum pasand nahi aaye to bata dijiye.* [If you do not like me, please tell me.]' It was the first sentence Satish uttered to her.

Sujata was instantly on the back foot. She said, 'No-no, seriously, Papa was around when you called in the morning, and then I had to rush for college. So I could not speak to you. Tell me.'

'I am leaving for my post today, so I thought of calling you.'

Sujata did not reply immediately. He hadn't left a great first impression on her. Nevertheless, they were in constant touch on the phone, which helped a great deal in breaking the ice between them. When Satish returned in April, with the intention to meet Sujata, he was a changed man. He did not meet her immediately. Rather, he enjoyed the extra pampering he received as the only child of the Dahiya family. Once his spirits rose again, he requested Sujata to meet him over lunch. She hesitated, but eventually agreed to the meeting at a restaurant near her college.

Like a scene out of a Bollywood movie, everything went in slow motion for her. A tall, fair, handsome man sauntered towards her. The signature Ray-Ban Aviators rested on his face. He looked impressive: from his shiny shoes to the crisp shirt neatly tucked inside his jeans. She was stunned. That was the first of their informal meetings before they were married a year later.

When she asked him shyly about his changed appearance during that period, he said, 'Sujata, I am the Company Commander of the Ghatak Platoon in my unit. I was on a forward post up on the mountains, and spent all my time out in the snow and the sun. I was not even really aware of our engagement ceremony; everything happened in a jiffy. I did not get any time to groom myself, but such is the life of every fauji. Our duty comes first, and everything else later.'

Then his face broke into a benevolent smile that created little wrinkles around his eyes and dimples in his cheeks. Sujata was thankful for the shades inside the restaurant. She fervently hoped that they hid her blushing cheeks. She also realized he was a humble man.

She still didn't know that the Ghatak Platoon or the 'lethal platoon' was a specialized army squad consisting of commandos. The Ghatak commandos are one of the finest, fastest, and deadliest troops of the unit provided with more advanced training than the regular soldiers. The advanced set of skills allow them to carry out extensive and risky operations like surgical strikes, assaulting enemy posts, bombing airfields, or directing air attacks or artillery fire. Though not Special Forces, Ghatak commandos can certainly be called as Special Forces of their own unit.

There was love, happiness, devotion, and a lot of bliss in the lives of the couple, though it was hard to believe when I visited her humble Separate Family Accomodation at Kargil Niwas in Dwarka. Inside the house the atmosphere was melancholic. The gloom in Sujata's eyes was heart-wrenching. One could make out that the woman in front was broken—someone who had lost everything in life.

Sujata once had a love story filled with many bright colours. Four-year-old Priyasha appeared from the adjacent room in a tiny little dress. She sat down quietly on one of the chairs, unlike children her age who usually do not rest for a second. Sujata held her by her hand and put her on her lap. I was at a loss for words. Not knowing what to say I gazed at the framed pictures on the wall, and said,

'You have lovely pictures here. The sari you wore looks gorgeous.'

She smiled an almost invisible smile. 'I thought now that he is not here, let me just put pictures of happier times on the wall.'

And there was silence in the room for a long time as we sat down. The story she shared might fill your eyes with tears and break your heart.

* * *

3 July 2012
Basantar Gali, Nowgam
Kashmir

Captain Satish had just taken out his phone—kept switched off in his uniform pocket for the past three days. It had been that long since the cordon-and-search operation where they went looking for terrorists. The tip-off was reliable, but even after three days they did not have any clue about them. The troops now believed that their source had been wrong, and restlessness among them was an indication that it was time to call off the operation. Satish thought of calling his new bride back at her maika—Pawera. He knew by now that Sujata would be worried. He had informed her about the ongoing operation, but had not had any time to call her.

'Hello Nikki,' he said, once she picked up the phone. He wanted some privacy while talking to his wife, whom he lovingly called Nikki. Fellow officers within earshot were already smirking. He started walking deep into the jungle.

'Why didn't you call me?' The new bride demanded. 'It has been three days, and everybody at home has been worried sick.'

'I told you I was involved in an operation. *Ab fauji se shaadi ki hai to iska nuksan bhi to uthana padega.* [Now that you have married a fauji, you will have to bear the trouble],' he teased her.

Before she could reply she heard the sound of a bullet shot on the phone, and the device switched off. Sujata panicked and informed her father, who panicked as well. It was only in the evening that Satish could call them again. Sujata cried with relief. Satish told her father how a bullet had been fired at him by one of the terrorists they had looked for for three days. The troops did not realize the terrorists were hiding deep inside the jungle, precisely at the spot Satish had unknowingly reached while talking on the phone.

One of the terrorists spotted him and fired in burst mode, but the bullet whizzed past a few inches over his head, and another struck his mobile phone—breaking it into pieces. Now aware of their positions, he hid behind a tree and called for backup. The encounter went on for a few more hours before all the three terrorists were neutralized. Later in the day, when they tried to move their bodies across Basantar Gali, heavy stone pelting started and a few stones hit Satish. Since he was injured, it took a while before he could reconnect with his wife.

It had only been five months of marriage. Sujata realized what it took to marry a man in olive green, and what it meant to be an Army wife. She stayed with her parents for quite a few months after their marriage. Satish served with the 1 Naga battalion, operating in a sensitive area near Nowgam in Kashmir, afflicted with heavy militancy. During his three-year attachment, he was a part of many successful operations. For one such daring operation, he was awarded the 'Chief of Army Staff Commendation Card' in 2013.

Talking to me Sujata said, 'The initial one year of our marriage was tough. Though I began to understand the challenges of his job immediately after our engagement—when days would go by without a phone call, or even without knowing his whereabouts—yet, it was only after the wedding that I could understand standing among the "silent ranks".' I could understand why the women behind our men are called tougher. They certainly need to have greater mental strength to deal with the life that comes after marrying the man in uniform. She continued, 'There was virtually no connection between us, and some days I would be worried to death. Sometimes I would feel he was ignoring me when, in reality, he was engaged in life-threatening operations. Sometimes he had to trudge up the steep hill slopes for mobile signals. My parents acted as my guiding light. My father had started taking particular interest in Kashmir. He knew about the activities of the security forces, and kept me posted. Those were difficult times for us all. I vividly remember the sleepless nights, when I was stuck in a time warp, waiting all the time, unable to focus on anything or carry on with my daily life.'

The tension-filled period of separation dissolved into the heavenly mist of Palampur, Himachal Pradesh, when

Satish was posted back to his corps unit 539 ASC battalion. Sujata joined him, and soon she was pregnant with Priyasha, who was born on 15 April 2014, at a Military Hospital in Yol Cantonment near Dharamshala. Sujata moved back to her parents in Pawera, Haryana, while Satish left for a course in Bangalore.

In 2015 Satish was posted to the 30 Rashtriya Rifles near Handwara, North Kashmir, where heavy infiltration by the Pakistani terrorists was a norm. He joined the 30 Rashtriya Rifles in March 2015, almost a year after their daughter was born. Sujata was apprehensive. She knew the drill of long-awaited phone calls, and fearing for his life, but she also knew how much Satish loved being in action.

She said to me, 'Satish was truly fascinated by Field Marshal Sam Manekshaw. He wanted to excel everywhere, just like him. He was also very particular about his uniform, and would not tolerate a single crease on it. The unit dhobi would be on his toes over his uniform. I knew he would not stop for our sake, no matter how much he loved Priyasha or me. Fighting against terrorists, alongside his troops, was his true calling.'

She also remembers how he would only talk about his operations and medals during their honeymoon in Kerala. She said, 'I used to be a small-town girl, and had never been out much. When I boarded my first flight to Kerala with him, I was elated beyond words. I was mesmerized by the enormousness of the Arabian Sea. We would sit on the beach for hours, while he narrated all kinds of stories about his operations. I did not understand anything, but I could make out his passion for his job.'

The times of great joy and merriment now feel like far-fetched fairy tales.

* * *

31 March 2015
Kupwara

Major Dahiya was confident about joining the 30 Rashtriya Rifles. The anxiety of entering a new unit, that too one as demanding as the Rashtriya Rifles, was not visible on his face. He had operated in the adjacent sector of Nowgam with the 1 Naga battalion two years ago, and he was well aware of the terrain. His Commanding Officer, Col Rajiv Saharan, was happy to receive the dynamic officer. He knew of his previous operations, and his commitment to the organization, beforehand. He had a hunch that this officer would bring laurels to the unit, and he was eager to trust him with challenging assignments matching his potential once he completed his compulsory training at the Corps Battle School.

After joining the 30 RR, Satish underwent the compulsory refresher training course at the School. These refresher training courses are orientation programmes, where the newly posted soldiers are taught about the unit's modus operandi, the terrain, the challenges, the weapons, and other advanced strategies. They are followed by rigorous physical tests and firing-proficiency tests. Satish excelled in all of them during the one-month training period.

After the completion of his course, he was given charge of Jungle Company as the Company Commander, and was deployed in the rural hinterland in a thick forest. He was also sent for the orientation programme regarding the battalions, like all officers usually were. He spent two or three days at each post, broadening his vision about the counter-insurgency operations going on in the area. It also provided him with an opportunity to mingle with the troops at the ground level, and learn the challenges they faced.

Satish was a people person. Friendly, jovial, and considerate, he soon established a rapport with the Company boys and officers of the 30 RR. He was also quite popular with the police personnel with whom he regularly carried out joint operations. His fearlessness and calm attitude also won the hearts of the locals who, for once, came forward by themselves to provide him information.

Cultivating a local informant is difficult, as Kashmiri locals hardly come forward fearing for their lives, but they knew Satish was an officer who would never let them down. He used his skills to develop a very reliable network of informants over his tenure, who proved very useful in the coming times and never failed him once.

Kashmir is a place where battles are won through intelligence networks. The more reliable your intelligence, the better the chances of your survival. It applies to both the sides—the soldiers and the terrorists.

The first thing Satish did was to ensure the complete safety, security, and comfort, of the men under him. He transformed the Company within no time.

He revolutionized the way fencings were done. He created a five-wall fencing system using useless Company stocks: punjis, wire, and broken-vehicle parts. They helped him develop a state-of-the-art baffle wall where the fatigued soldiers could sleep without any worry.

Within no time his Company Operating Base (COB) was the most secure of all. He was always very considerate towards the happiness and morale of his troops. Soon, his Company boys surrendered their loyalty and faith to him. They knew this officer would put himself first in the line of danger and duty both.

The year 2015 went as a very successful year for the 30 RR. The unit won them many laurels for their daring operations involving Hizbul Mujahideen, Lashkar-e-Taiba, and Jaish-e-Mohammed terrorist groups. Some of their missions were also highlighted by the then Minister of External Affairs, Late Smt. Sushma Swaraj, in the UN assembly sessions.[9]

Major Dahiya held deep affection and concern for his parents. Despite operating under extraordinary situations, and immense pressure, never once did he back out of his duties as the only child. He went to attend his cousin's wedding in May 2015, where he developed acute pain in the abdomen, later diagnosed as appendicitis. He was instantly referred to R&R Hospital, Delhi, for surgery. Once a soldier has been operated, he is declared as low in the medical category, and unfit for active operations. That was the window where Major Dahiya could have returned to his corps unit at a peace station, opting out of the 30 Rashtriya Rifles, and no one would have objected. But he knew his calling was in the thick Kashmiri jungles where death loomed at every corner, and the terrorists never allowed the soldiers to sleep well.

Did those obstacles ever matter to the passionate officer? No. It was not for nothing that he wrote over his extra-secure bunker, 'I rust when I rest.'

The CO, too, was not willing to relieve one of his best Company Commanders. Instead of taking up the case, and demanding a fitter officer, he designated Satish as Adjutant of the unit and put him on staff duties. Satish also proved his mettle. He did not rest a day, but worked diligently. He utilized that time to perform all his staff duties excellently, and established an informant network. He would also stay awake during the night-time operations, even though it was not necessary.

The then 30 RR Commanding Officer, Col Rajiv Saharan, remembers how such officers are assets to the organization, and the tales of their selfless service to the nation inspire an entire generation of new soldiers joining the unit during tough times.

* * *

21 September 2015
Banihari
Haryana

Sujata, at her in-laws' place, was troubled and irritated, which was unusual for her calm-and-composed nature. It was Satish's birthday the next day, 22 September, and she wanted to make him feel special, even if she was not there with him to celebrate the big day. She talked to the Quarter Master, Col Punj, many times, and also to Satish's buddy, to ask if they could arrange a small surprise cake for him, along with a bouquet. They pleaded helplessness, as they feared a cake from outside could be easily poisoned, and there was no way to bake a cake at a field station.

Eventually, the buddy promised Sujata that he would present Satish a bouquet once he woke up early in the morning. On 22 September, around 6.00 a.m., Sujata received Satish's call. Talking on the phone at unearthly hours was a routine between the couple.

'Hello,' she said.

Happy laughter filled the phone. Satish was laughing loudly.

Sujata pretended to be annoyed, and said, 'Finish laughing first, then call me. What is this—calling so early in the day and laughing so much?'

'I am sorry. Hahaha . . . oh! I am sorry, but I just cannot control my laughter. Tell me, whose idea was it to present me with a bouquet on my birthday?'

'Mine, of course. Who else's? I have been stressing over arranging things for your birthday for the past one week. You don't know how much effort I put in to make you feel special on your birthday—only because I care . . . not like you who, instead of extending thanks, are laughing.'

'No-no, I am truly touched. But why did you ask for a dry-flower bouquet, which looks rather dusty? Perhaps it was taken from an old vase from the mess?' He laughed again.

Later it was revealed that because of security protocols Satish's buddy could not arrange fresh flowers, and had eventually tied some dry flowers from an old vase from the mess together for Major Dahiya. He had presented the bouquet to him first thing in the morning as he had promised Sujata.

Later in November that year, Sujata visited Satish for some days, with Priyasha. Even though conflicts ravaged Kashmir, Sujata found it magnificent and revelatory. The enchanting scenery and tranquillity, where she could never step out without protection, is still etched in her heart. In the comfort of their little guest house Satish would serve her piping hot Kahwa sprinkled with Kashmiri kesar and almonds. Then there were world-famous Kashmiri walnuts, which he insited on breaking himself before offering them to her. They were regular couple things but, for the two people forced to stay away, it was a lifetime of loving and caring. Once they even sneaked out to take a shikara ride on the pristine silver-blue waters of the Dal Lake, breaking the security protocol. It was the day she was to return home.

She remembers how Satish played with Priyasha at the officers' mess. Both of them would run behind rabbits, and Satish eventually caught the tiny little creatures just for his daughter to touch. Priyasha went running around in the mess garden, her favourite hobby, plucking flowers from the carefully manicured lawn. Those memories have not faded yet, and may never be erased from her memory.

* * *

July 2016
Kashmir

A brief encounter of Hizbul Mujahideen Commander, Burhan Wani, sparked unrest in the Valley. He was one of the modern terrorists, who believed in utilizing the power of social media to radicalize and recruit the gullible local youth. His death resulted in riots, stone pelting, protests, and deadly attacks on the security forces by his supporters. The security forces retaliated. It caught the attention of the international media, and the enemy country also tried to defame India.

For the security personnel deployed there it was a challenging situation to keep peace, using mimimal force and avoiding civilian casualties. The Indian Army deployed various teams to control the situation, who worked in close coordination with the police and other paramilitary forces. Major Satish Dahiya was a part of one such team.

Col Rajiv Saharan remembers the time. To me he said, 'Satish handled the situation maturely. I did not hear of a single incident of mischief or mismanagement from his area. He was a great combatant, and also an exceptional team leader, with excellent people-management skills. His death was a great loss to the unit and also to the Army.'

Sujata worried about Satish those days. He would call her during the night inspections, and during the security rounds after midnight, and say, 'Sujata, if anything happens to any of my men, I don't know how I will face their families. I also hope Kashmir regains its normality soon. I am giving it my best.'

Sujata had always been a tremendous support to him, and she would console him. She said to me, 'I remember the time when I visited him in Kashmir. Whenever he returned from his regular cordon-and-search operations, his fauji boots would always be covered with ice and snow. His feet would be ice-cold, almost numb, and he would sit across from the two kerosene heaters in the room the whole time. I wondered if he ever had the time to get back to his room and sit in front of the heater those days, but I never asked him. Not that it mattered to him. He had a job to do.'

The turmoil gradually abated and, to an extent, peace returned to the Valley but, for Satish, new challenges were surfacing. His reliable informants informed him about the presence of foreign terrorists from JeM—the Afzal Guru Squad—in his area.

The Afzal Guru Squad was a fidayeen squad—made of battle-hardened terrorists who had received commando training on a par with the Special Forces. The information was that four Pakistani terrorists had entered India, and had taken over as terrorist Commanders of the general area. They were developing a blueprint to create chaos and damage in the Valley. They had ambushed many Army convoys, and carried out attacks, inflicting casualties on them in the past.[10] Satish knew the gravity of the situation, and how important it was to neutralize them.

Col Saharan mentioned he once said to Satish, during a mess party, rather casually, 'I am due for a posting, and you will also leave in a few months. However, if a bright and young officer like you leaves without a good mission, I will be disappointed.'

That was of course said on a lighter note, but Satish took it rather personally. He pushed his resources to find the Afzal Guru Squad roaming freely in the area creating disturbance. He knew very well that if not neutralized on time, they were capable of creating havoc.

On 14 February 2017, an informant confirmed to the CO, Col Saharan, that the terrorists were present in Hajin Kralgund village. The CO 30 Rashtriya Rifles, and his men, laid out an excellent plan for the cordon-and-search operation. This was a joint operation with the Jammu and Kashmir police. The particular terrorists had recently bombed a police station, and the police were also on the lookout for them.

Initially, Major Dahiya, who was involved with other operation, was not supposed to be a part of that particular operation that day. However, since the military and paramilitary forces work in close coordination in Kashmir, and are well acquainted with each other, Sub-divisional Police Officer, Handwara Shabir Khan, who was well acquainted with Major Dahiya, requested the Commanding Officer to include him in the exercise. Both of them knew about Satish's close pursuit of the terrorists, and he was included to lead the operation at the last minute.

SDPO Sabir Khan also remembers an incident when one of their friends received a Shaurya Chakra, and Major Dahiya jokingly mentioned earning a bigger medal soon. He said, 'He didn't know then that he would not win just the medal, but the hearts of 1.3 billion Indians, having made the supreme sacrifice.'[11]

Amidst everything Satish also planned a surprise gift for Sujata, to be delivered precisely on Valentine's Day.

He didn't know either that it would be his last gift to her. He called her several times that day, regarding the Valentine gift due to be delivered.

A colleague of his told me how often he mentioned his family, and expressed his worries over their future if something happened to him. He was aware of the risks involved in his work, and he cared deeply about his wife, and daughter Priyasha—whom he called the light of his life. His performance as a soldier and as an officer, though, was never affected by the sentiments of a father and a husband.

Sujata had moved to Jaipur just a month ago, and taken a Separate Family Accomodation (SFA)[12] as soon as it was clear that he would be posted to the same city within a few months. She expected the courier once she returned home after picking up her daughter from kindergarten at noon. She was excited to receive the gift, and wanted to open it as soon as possible, utterly unaware of Satish's situation. For her the operation was routine. Never for a second did she expect that the future would bring such grief and void in her life.

* * *

14 February 2017
'Aaj Muqabala Hoga'
Hajin Kralgund
Kashmir

Hajin Kralgund was a small village with several families staying in compact houses. Women and children went on with their daily lives. The Indian Army was ethically bound to prevent civilian casualties, and any such operation in and around residential areas had huge risks of such fatalities. A well-planned strategy was chalked out, comprising two cordon parties. The joint team swung into action and the operation started around 5.00 p.m. As per the intelligence inputs, the militants were holed up in a residential building.

The outer cordon led by Commanding Officer, Col Saharan, of the 30 RR, received live video feed from a quadcopter drone in a small operation room, keeping a watch over the whole operation. The outer cordon was meant to prevent escapes, and provide backup when needed, without drawing much attention.

The inner cordon was divided into two parties, one led by Major Dahiya around the suspicious house, and the other by a JCO at the edge of the village. The cordon parties were smaller in number, but doubly effective tactically, a perfectly laid cordon that ensured minimum casualties.

Sub-divisional Police Officer, Sabir Khan, also mentioned how Major Dahiya said, 'Aaj muqabla hoga,' before leaving for the operation. And, when Sabir expressed his doubts, Dahiya told him to keep the faith—because faith was what kept the Tricolour flying high.[13]

Many a time squads return to base, or wait for hours over false intel, or patrol parties roam around in jungles for months over vague inputs, in the hope of some contact with the millitants. It is strange how Major Dahiya was so accurate about the contact.

The Major and his men received a volley of bullets from AK-47 machine guns once they reached the suspicious house on the edge of the village. Out of four terrorists, one had broken the cordon and escaped into the forest, but the three others were still trapped inside. In sheer desperation they resorted to indiscriminate firing against the troops.

The Forces rapidly took position and returned fire. Major Dahiya and his buddy sneaked into the compound, while the other soldiers kept the terrorists engaged in a gunfight. Both of them spotted a small mound of earth and took cover behind it. Precisely at the moment the three terrorists, in an attempt to flee, burst through the front door firing indiscriminately.

A little distraction of a fraction of seconds—and one of the bullets found Satish. Though he was in his military gear, and wore a bulletproof vest, it was only a matter of fate that the bullet found its way through the gap between two plates, ripping a major artery at the bottom of his heart. But it did not bother him, and he continued firing back.

One terrorist had been neutralized by now, but the other two found cover and went on firing. They also sent several grenades towards the periphery of the compound, which hit three of the soldiers—providing cover fire to Satish and his buddy. Satish instantly asked for assistance for their evacuation, but refused it for himself. At that moment he could have saved his own life rather than kill the terrorists. He knew they were capable of breaking the cordon to escape into the jungle under the circumstances. He also knew they could cause more deaths and destruction with their high morale. They needed to be neutralized even at the cost of his life. Satish chose to neutralize those dreaded terrorists over his own life.

The Commanding Officer had joined the inner cordon by now, and deployed men all around. He asked Satish to leave but, again, Satish refused. Soon he eliminated one more terrorist. The third terrorist, while desperately trying to escape, was killed in an encounter minutes later by the outer-cordon troops. With the encounter coming to an end, the men found Satish all soaked in blood. He was evacuated immediately.

Major Dahiya was a people person. The news spread—and everybody from the locals to the police personnel, to the neighbouring fauji units, flooded his unit for the news of his well-being. The pilots of the Army Aviation Squadron, many of whom knew him personally because of his daredevil attitude, willingly volunteered for a daring operation in the middle of the night—to fly across the thick forests of northern Kashmir for the evacuation. They knew losing the hero, who valued his motherland above everything else, would be a huge loss for them all.

Meanwhile, back in Jaipur, Sujata had not received the parcel yet, and her restlessness grew. She had called Satish several times, but he never answered. It was already dark. Though it was not for the first time that Satish hadn't picked up his phone, somehow she could feel the apprehension wrapping her soul. Her heart was sinking to unknown depths. She tried to call Satish a few more times, and the phone rang silently in his pocket while he fought bravely, displaying exemplary leadership and courage.[14]

Satish succumbed to his gunshot injury during the evacuation. The renowned doctors at 92 base hospital could not save him. Somewhere around that time the doorbell at Sujata's house rang, and the courier delivered the much-awaited Valentine's gift, a heart-shaped cake and a red-rose bouquet—which she placed on the dining table affectionately, and called Satish one more time. The phone rang silently in his pocket as he breathed his last, dying like a hero over the beautiful Kashmiri lands he loved—and where he had found his true calling.

People say the soul is neither created nor destroyed. It is eternal and knows everything past, present, and future. The knowledge is buried deep inside the subconsciousness of a human being. Perhaps Satish's soul had planned centuries ago how he would depart, bidding a proper goodbye to the love of his life.

His last message to Sujata said, 'Nikki, I love you.' It was written beautifully on the little card accompanying the bouquet.

By 8.30 p.m. Sujata started receiving a flurry of calls from Major Dahiya's colleagues, who confirmed that Satish had been shot, but said there was nothing to worry about. The wife of the warrior lit a diya in her small mandir with utmost faith, and prayed like a true fighter herself. She did not allow a single tear to roll down her eyes.

I remember how her faith in God is still intact, and how she motivated me to celebrate Karwa Chauth in 2019, when my own husband was not well and I held a grudge against the Gods. She said, 'Things could be much worse. If not anything else, praying will give you peace.'

I understood what kind of an incredible woman Satish had chosen as his life partner. No one could have been a better match than her for the warrior who breathed not air but courage.

Meanwhile, Col Saharan called Satish's uncle and requested him to break the news to the family. He also called Sujata's father and asked him to reach Jaipur at the earliest. Sujata knew—the moment she found her shaken father at her doorstep—and sat down in shock. The joint operation was a huge mission, and the news soon broke on television as well. People started pouring condolences on social media.

An Army Major from Satish's unit, on leave in Jaipur, reached Sujata's house and assisted them in every possible manner. En-route to Srinagar Sujata still hoped against hope for Satish's well-being. Then she received a call from Col Saharan. Priyasha was on her lap. With a voice much shaken with grief the CO informed them about Satish's 'veergati', and asked her to be strong to be able to take care of Priyasha and herself.

The world blanked out for several minutes as her father changed their course and turned towards Banihari, the village where Satish's parents lived. A huge crowd, chanting slogans in Satish's glory, had already gathered across the roads around the area, at his residence, and everywhere else. The news had spread. People wanted to pay homage to their hero. There was already an entire battalion of the Army assisting the family in every way. Prime Minister Narendra Modi also paid tribute to Major Satish Dahiya. Such was the glory of the supreme sacrifice made by him.[15]

In the evening the next day, when the Tiranga-wrapped casket reached his home, loud chants pierced the air. Sujata, who had clutched the cake and the bouquet the moment she had left Jaipur, cried to the depths of her being. Her grief brought tears to the eyes of the whole nation.

Priyasha, the one-and-a-half-year-old, did not understand a thing but lit her father's pyre. That moment pushed people to cry loudly. This responsibility was too big for her tiny shoulders. But Priyasha, the daughter of a brave soldier, did it with utmost grace and calm.

Two days after the funeral, on her wedding anniversary, Sujata learnt that Satish had booked Taj Vivanta in Goa for their daughter's second birthday celebrations in April. They had planned a beach holiday many times in the past. She never knew until that time that Satish had taken those wishes for a beach vacation seriously, and wanted to surprise her.

For days she cried until her tears dried up and she slumped on a chair, closing her eyes for some time, only to get up and cry again. She lost track of time for a long while, and eventually had to be put on antidepressants. Her mother and her sister looked after her daughter during that time.

Later Sujata moved to Delhi—to a Separate Family Accomodation (SFA), where she currently stays. The Indian Army has a provision for a separate family accommodation to a grieving veer nari for some years, which allows her a smooth transition to normal life after her husband's sudden demise. The Haryana state government also helped Major Dahiya's family a lot. They even offered a job to Sujata, which she had joined by the time this book was published. She also told me how she intended to make a difference through her position, just like her husband did. Priyasha is now five years old, and still thinks her father is on duty. Sujata plans to tell her the truth soon.

Satish's parents have lost their zeal to live after losing their only child. They find solitude in social work in the name of their son, who has acquired the stature of a legend in the village. A road and a school have been named after him by the state government. Even a stadium has been erected in his memory. The 30 Rashtriya Rifles renovated their war memorial right after Major Dahiya's martyrdom, and engraved his name on it in a grand event. They also named their gym after him for the troops. His busts have also been placed at 539 ASC battalion, Palampur, and the ASC Regimental Centre, Bangalore, where he had once trained—and inspires a whole lot of new soldiers today.

* * *

This story is based on the conversation with Mrs Sujata Chaudhary, wife of Major Satish Dahiya; and Col Rajiv Saharan, the then Commanding Officer of the 30 Rashtriya Rifles. Some serving soldiers from the Major's platoon, who were a part of that operation but wish to remain anonymous over security reasons, also helped. Major Dahiya was commissioned in 2009 as an ASC Officer, and was the only officer from his area. However, after his 'veergati', his tales of valour inspired many to join the Forces as officers. For his unmatched gallantry, and his supreme sacrifice while fighting the militants, Major Dahiya was posthumously awarded the Shaurya Chakra, the third in the order of precedence of peacetime gallantry awards.[16] Sujata has joined office as the Excise and Taxation Officer in the Excise and Taxation Department, Haryana—a job offered to her by Haryana Government. Little Priyasha also keeps her occupied. Occasionally, she wears her dad's uniform and looks exactly like him.

Two Bodies, One Soul

Sarika Gulati and Lt Col Rajesh Gulati
Sena Medal (P)

'Hello, Mote! How are you? I am leaving for a sortie. Will be back in an hour.'

Sarika could hear the sound of the enormous rotor blades of the Dhruv helicopter on the phone. It was an indigenously-built Advanced Light Helicopter—a twin-engine aircraft manufactured by the government-owned Hindustan Aeronautics Limited. Her husband, Lt Col Rajesh Gulati, was on an anti-terrorist operation, his chopper acting as an aerial observation platform for the Rashtriya Rifles in Safapura Heights in northern Kashmir. Accompanying him was the young budding pilot, Major Tahir Hussain Khan,[17] on that fateful day—11 February 2015.

It was their code of conduct. Lt Col Gulati knew Sarika panicked if he did not call her before and after his sorties.

Around 600 kilometres away in her rented flat in Dwarka, Delhi, Sarika had been feeling low that day. There was trepidation in her heart. She felt drained of her usual energy. Except for her instincts she felt absolutely fine. Her health was normal; the air was pleasantly cool—typical of Delhi winters—and Saksham, their twelve-year-old son, looked joyful.

Sarika even refused the class with the tabla instructor, who visited them thrice a week for tabla lessons. On regular days it was perhaps the most exciting task for her, while her husband served at Manasbal, Kashmir, a field station. She smiled feebly when she found Saksham trying to master the tabla beats merrily across the room, but she could not gather the strength to join him.

Lt Col Rajesh Gulati was her Raj whom she had fondly named after the character of Shahrukh Khan in the '90s superhit, *Dilwale Dulhniya Le Jayenge,* literally: 'The Brave-hearted shall Carry the Bride Away'. It was almost her own story. The quintessential shy girl next door, who belongs to a traditional family, finally falls for a flippant, cool guy who crosses every limit, travels across the world, gets beaten, and braves all odds to win her over. An impossible love.

She smiled for once that day when the flashback revived the old memories locked away carefully.

* * *

1995
Prem Nagar
Dehradun

Rajesh Gulati and Sarika Dang were neighbours. Sarika had grown up in a joint family comprising her grandparents, aunts, uncles, and cousins, sharing the bonding and bonhomie of a typical close-knit family of the '90s. She had had a memorable and secure childhood. Their cohesive force had given her strong family values and also reservations.

She was every inch unlike Rajesh Gulati—the next-door neighbour who lived in a nuclear family, bossing his two younger brothers around. His father, Sri Kundan Lal Gulati, was a high-ranking official at the Oil and Natural Gas Corporation (ONGC), Dehradun; and his mother, Smt. Asha Gulati, was the quintessential Punjabi woman busy running her house. Rajesh had spent a significant part of his school and college life back in Prem Nagar, guiding, mentoring, and helping the neighbourhood children who dropped in every evening for free tuitions.

Sarika Dang, who occupied a back seat in his spacious drawing room, along with her cousins, would always bring a sparkle in his eyes, and he could hear his heart beat. Take it as an emotional hangover of the '90s infatuation, where the crush was not just a crush but a deity. They had known each other since they were babies but, it was only in 1995, when Sarika was in the eleventh standard and Rajesh in BSc first year, that they could feel an attraction between them and started dating.

They would go for long morning walks at Tea Garden, Prem Nagar, with Sarika's cousins. Sarika would sometimes make the morning tea for Rajesh. Rajesh's mother had known Sarika since she was crawling on all fours, and it was not unusual for her to find her barging into the house at unearthly hours.

In the afternoons Rajesh would visit Moravian School on Rajput Road, where Sarika studied. He would bunk his college, wait for hours, pick up Sarika once her school was over, and both would walk down to her bus stop. That was the only time when they were indeed alone. They would open their hearts to each other, share their secrets, and laugh out loud. Sometimes he would also hold her hands. Sarika felt loved, and secure with him at that tender age.

Rajesh was not just her lover but also a friend, mentor, and guide. In the evenings he taught her along with the other children the subjects in which they lagged behind their peers. Rajesh would wipe her tears when she was upset, make her laugh when she felt low, and listen patiently to all her problems regarding school. They were two bodies, one soul. Their hearts beat as one, but they also knew their parents would not take their relationship kindly.

Recently, they had started meeting on Sarika's terrace. It was not a regular practice but, whenever Sarika felt troubled, she would request Rajesh to meet her there. He would jump onto her terrace from his own. She clearly remembers the night of 2 December 1996. It was her parents' wedding anniversary. The aroma of exquisite Punjabi food—dal makhani, chole, and paneer butter masala, had enveloped the house. All the children in the house were excited. Sometimes, they would run and open the kitchen door impatiently. There was a festive feeling at home.

When the elaborate family dinner began in the dining area, the air was filled with laughter and warmth. The cousins were happily devouring the generously laid dinner, and the dry fruit-loaded moong daal halwa made Sarika anxious. All she could think of was how Raj would love to have the piping hot halwa in that cold. She hid a small bowlful of the dessert under her dupatta and sneaked out. Once she reached the terrace, she quickly threw a little stone into Rajesh's room. It was around 9.00 p.m. She knew he would be studying in his room.

Rajesh took the hint. He reached his terrace and jumped onto Sarika's.

'I brought you halwa,' she almost whispered.

'Wow! I just had my dinner, and I was craving for some sweet. How do you always know what I want?' He took the bowl and savoured it happily.

They stood holding each other, smelling the sweet aroma of marigold and listening to the night sounds of the laidback Prem Nagar that was just about to retire for the day.

But the world was blissful only for a few seconds. Rajesh heard footsteps coming up and instantly jumped over to his terrace. Sarika turned around, and found her furious mother, who had come searching for her. Mothers' instincts aren't usually wrong. She stood staring at Sarika.

'Who was he?' she growled.

'Who, Ma?' Sarika shivered.

'Don't try to fool me. I just saw somebody jumping off our terrace. Who was he?' she seethed.

'I don't know what you are talking—' The sentence could not be completed. Her mother slapped her hard.

Tears ran down Sarika's cheeks, taking on the dark colour of her kajal. She had never been hit before, but she did not say anything. Her mother kept asking about the boy she had just seen her daughter with, but Sarika did not utter a word. Her mother picked up a stick and started thrashing her. Sarika had never seen her like that. Her mother could not digest the secret meeting of her teenage daughter with someone, right under their noses. She knew the consequences of living in a joint family. She knew that if the family ever learnt about it, they would not take it well.

Sarika cried without uttering a word. Rajesh meant everything to her. Her mother finally surrendered to her daughter's stubbornness. Tired, she held her by her hand and took her downstairs. Another person wept on the adjacent terrace at that time—Rajesh!

He felt loved. He felt fortunate to have Sarika in his life. The sheer intensity of her emotions was overwhelming. It filled his heart not just with deep regret, but also with deep love.

Sarika was grounded for two days, though her mother did not spill the beans to anyone, including her father. She was their only daughter and, despite everything, she loved her a lot. She also felt guilty about hitting her in the heat of the moment. It was also the reason she did not react when Rajesh visited her after a few days.

He touched her feet, put his palms together, and said, 'Aunty, you wanted to know about the boy with Sarika? It was me. I love Sarika very much, and she loves me too. One day I am going to marry her and, till then, I want you to keep her safe for me.'

He tried to touch her feet once more, but the seething mother moved away. He put his palms together once again, and walked out of her house. Things had changed for him now. He wanted to become something—someone Sarika's mother would consider worthy enough for her daughter.

It was also the time when Rajesh had appeared for the Pilot Aptitude Battery Test (PABT), and cleared it, but his mother was reluctant to send him to the Air Force, considering it too risky. He had always been interested in the Armed Forces. He knew it was embedded deep in his heart. He wanted to become a soldier and serve the nation. His proximity to IMA, Dehradun, also played a massive role in shaping his decision to become an officer. Later, apart from a BSc from DAV College, Dehradun, he also applied for the CDS examinations for the Army.

He continued meeting Sarika until his mother, too, came to know about their relationship. One day a common friend caught them at the Prem Nagar temple, and informed Sarika's mother, Asha Gulati. When Sarika reached home, she could feel something was not right. She found Rajesh's mother sitting inside with her mother and aunt. They looked tense, while Asha Gulati looked furious.

'*Lo ji, aa gayi aapki laadli. Mere bete pe dore dalne ke baad*. [Look, your daughter's back after trying to seduce my son],' Rajesh's mother taunted hers.

'Please don't say that. My daughter is very innocent. Your son loves her,' her mother said hesitantly.

'How dare you! It is your daughter, and you should leash her. Next time I find her with my son, I will ensure I make her life hell.' Rajesh's mother was a typical doting Punjabi woman. She felt betrayed by her son, and Sarika whom she had always welcomed at her place. She was livid and distraught.

That was the last day of 'Happy Days at Prem Nagar' for the couple. The bliss of morning walks, bed teas, and the happiness of evening tuitions soon faded into the chaos of family rivalries. Both families, once friends, were now against each other and fought like cats and dogs.

The CDS exam results were announced. Rajesh had cleared it as expected. He was soon to join IMA, Dehradun. But all that mattered to him was Sarika's well-being. He knew the moment he left, her life would turn into hell. He also wanted to diffuse the family tension. He asked Sarika to move out of Prem Nagar, and take admission somewhere else. Sarika shifted to Delhi to pursue BCom.

* * *

June 1996
IMA, Dehradun

Rajesh Gulati looked up at the imposing gates ahead and sighed, as a bead of sweat trickled down his cheek. He stood at the verge of realizing his dream. The proximity of his house to the IMA had allowed him an intimate view into the lives of the Gentlemen Cadets, one that had convinced him that this was his true calling. His excitement and nervous anticipation was tempered by the realization that the strict fitness regimen, soon to follow, would challenge him to the hilt. A brilliant student, who had achieved exceptional school grades with little effort, he knew he would have to dig his heels in if he was to stand any chance of keeping up with ex-NDA cadets. They would join his batch soon—already physically and mentally conditioned to the military regime.

Barely a few months into the first term, Raj had established himself as one of the more popular guys in Keren Company. Ever willing to help others, he was always bothered with queries from course mates and seniors alike about the happening places in Dehradun to spend a weekend 'Liberty' or an 'out pass' off-campus. Sometimes, his course mates would also raid his house to devour home-made food.

As he had initially reckoned, the fitness regimen at the Academy challenged everyone, but especially the Direct Entry Gentlemen Cadets, who had had no previous taste of such physical conditioning. Raj met the challenge head-on. From eighty-plus kilograms, he dropped into a comfortable range of the sixties, and put in extra hours and toil in dealing with the dreaded nemesis of many DEs, the BPET.

On 13 June 1998, Raj slow marched across the Antim Pag in the hallowed Chetwood Block with the 102nd Regular Course, and was commissioned as an officer in the 110 Medium Regiment—the Regiment of Artillery. Sarika was also about to complete her BCom from the University of Dehi.

* * *

1999
Arunachal Pradesh

Rajesh joined the Artillery, and his first posting was in Arunanchal Pradesh. His mother started pressurizing him for marriage, and pushed him to meet several girls. Sarika and Rajesh's families had still not stopped fighting. They were on more bitter terms than before. There was also a time when he almost gave up on Sarika and called to tell her that.

'Hi, Mote! How are you?' It was his opening sentence whenever he called her.

'I am good. Thank you for calling. I was missing you terribly,' Sarika replied in her usual chirpy tone.

Rajesh did not say anything for a few moments. Then he said, 'Sarika, I called to break up with you. We left Prem Nagar to dissolve the tensions between the families, but nothing has been resolved. My mom does not keep well. She went through a lot to raise us. I cannot disappoint her all the time. She has introduced me to this girl, Minu, who she thinks will be perfect for me. I have no energy left to convince her about you once more. Even my brothers are pushing me to marry this girl.'

Sarika was in tears. She put the phone down quietly. Rajesh did not call her for another fifteen days. It was the longest period when they had not talked. She was heartbroken, but she received his call on sixteenth day. He swore to his love and affection for her, and said, 'Whatever happens now, I'll make it clear to my family that only you can be my wife, or else I will never marry. Let's go to Dehradun together. Let's get married.'

Sarika was relieved, but also scared about this sudden marriage proposal. She knew how their families hated each other, and how Rajesh's mother disliked her, but there was no way out. And now she could neither turn back nor hold on any longer. They both reached Dehradun and pursued their parents determinedly. Eventually, the parents bowed before their children's wishes. Rajesh rushed to Sarika the moment he heard the news.

'*Mote! humari shaadi ho rahi hai. Ghar wale maan gaye hai. Ab to khush ho na?* [Fatso, we're getting married. The families have agreed. Happy now?]' he said, overjoyed.

Sarika started crying. 'How?' she murmured. 'How did it happen?'

'They fought the whole day, but now they have agreed to our marriage. Let's go for the Roka,' he said.

'What! Roka? Now? I am not even prepared,' she stammered, thinking no other woman in the world must have been engaged like this.

'It does not matter. Come.' Rajesh took her back to his house, and they exchanged rings in the presence of their family members. The marriage date was decided for April 2000.

How she wishes now she had had a hint of what lay in the future. Then maybe she could have planned things better, laughed more, cried less, and cherished every single second of it.

* * *

15 April 2000
Dehradun

The Dang and Gulati families forgot everything and began the wedding revelries in the most boisterous manner.

A grand cocktail party was hosted at the boy's residence, followed by the whimsical but charming Punjabi wedding ceremonies.

The two were wed in an evening ceremony that boasted magnificent decor, matching outfits, and loads of fun. On the wedding day Sarika was undeniably the cynosure of all eyes. She slipped into her maroon-and-gold bridal attire, and paired it with the most gorgeous jewellery-ensemble. Rajesh looked handsome in his cream-and-beige sherwani. He already carried stars on his shoulders, but that day he had stars in his eyes as well.

On their honeymoon they spent hours on Brigade Road in Bangalore, cherishing the metro vibes. In Ooty, they explored the vast tea plantations and meadows, towering mountains, the pine and eucalyptus trees, sparkling waterfalls, and the serene lakes. Some days they would not even go outside, but watch the sunset together from their hotel suite, over a steaming cup of coffee, wrapped in each other's arms. Then there was a heavenly boat ride on the shimmering waters with the surrounding greenery at Kodaikanal, before they returned to Prem Nagar, where Rajesh dropped Sarika and left for his Artillery unit, 110 Medium Regiment, based in Ambala. Sarika, now a Gulati bahu, stayed with her mother-in-law for the time being.

Rajesh asked Sarika to join him at Ambala after a month. On a hot June morning she, as a new bride, reached the Ambala station to start her life as a fauji wife. She was overwhelmed to find all her husband's unit officers and ladies waiting to receive her. With much respect she was escorted to the two-room bachelor's accommodation at

Ambala Cantonment, but everybody vanished even before she could say thank you, or begin with formal introductions.

She found it weird but kept quiet, being a civilian with absolutely no exposure to Defence life. She was not sure about what to expect. She also found Rajesh leaving hurriedly soon after, though he asked her to be ready for lunch at the mess. And he insisted that she should dress up as a bride even in that heat.

A corner of her heart was a little disappointed. She muttered under her breath, 'This is what happens when you get married. All men are the same.'

Already loaded with her bridal gold jewellery, Sarika dressed carefully in a new sari in that hot-and-humid weather. A smart Junior Officer, Lt Rajpurohit, appeared at her doorstep by noon and asked her to accompany him. Dazed, she waited alone for around two hours at that officer's house. He had also vanished soon after leaving her there. Next she met a lady, who informed her that 'Captain Gulati' had met with an accident and was waiting for her at the Officers' Mess. Nervous, Sarika rushed to the mess where she found Rajesh smiling ear-to-ear, all covered in bandages. He was with all the unit officers and their wives, sitting around on the couches.

Right when she was about to break into tears, the Commanding Officer's wife, Mrs Malini Edward, rushed and hugged her. Everybody broke into laughter. Rajesh, too, removed his fake bandages and joined in the laughter. It was a joke played on her. The Indian Army has a culture of treating the 'lady wives' with utmost respect but, when a newly wedded officer's wife enters the tribe, several age-old military traditions of welcoming her in a unique way are practised. They might sometimes be nerve-racking for her, only to turn into memories of a lifetime later. The newly-weds were made to cut the cake, and Rajesh smeared it on her face. After a hearty lunch the couple was made to sit on a decorated fauji sand truck with 'newly-married' written over it, which eventually dropped them at their accommodation.

Sarika remembers the day well. She said with a chuckle, 'That was how I was welcomed into this crazy tribe. I was hugely pampered in the Army family. The Second-in-command, my 2IC's wife—Mrs K.J. Singh, and my CO's wife—Mrs Malini Edward, taught me many things military. They also told me that Rajesh had a challenging job, and I should be aware of my role as an Army wife, as it concerned the nation's safety as well as my husband's. They also made me realize my duties towards the jawans' families—and why I needed to be there for them. We were one big family away from the family. Those memories as a new bride still warm my heart. There would be lunches, dinners, get-togethers, and whatnot.'

* * *

9 October 2002
Allahabad

Rajesh was out on a sortie when the ATC informed his co-pilot about the good news. Sarika had just delivered a healthy baby boy back at Dehradun. The cockpit suddenly converted into a happy place, as the flooding congratulatory messages lifted 'everybody's mood. Almost immediately Rajesh boarded an Army aircraft heading towards Delhi. Such were the perks of his job. He did not need tickets to reach his family when he wished. From Delhi he boarded a bus to Dehradun and, at 6.00 a.m. the next day, he was standing in front of a surprised Sarika on her hospital bed, holding their baby.

As soon as Saksham turned two months old, Sarika joined Rajesh at Kanchrapara, West Bengal, where he had just been posted. Together they set up their little fauji accommodation as comfortably as they could for a baby. The house was painted in bright colours, and hundreds of toys were bought. They felt they had conquered the world. Little Saksham strengthened their bond further.

* * *

2009
Nashik

The newly inducted Advanced Light Helicopter (ALH)-Dhruv[18] hovered unsteadily over the helipad, unable to maintain a safe height or direction. Sweat trickled down Lt Col Sunil Das's forehead. He had been newly posted as the Instrumental Rating (IR) pilot, the number two in the chain of command in a flight of the ALH Army Aviation Squadron at Nashik.[19] He was an experienced pilot himself, but he had only flown the single-engine Cheetah and Chetek helicopters earlier. The multi-engine and multi-feature Dhruv was proving to be a challenge for him. He was particularly uncomfortable with the advanced flight-control systems of the aircraft.

At this very instant, Major Rajesh Gulati, the youngest Qualified Flying Instructor (QFI), and one among the first-generation of officers to have trained on these Dhruv helicopters, barked out instructions to his pupil over the intercommunication system: 'Sir! Please depress the trim releases and wait for the aircraft to respond. You have to trust the aircraft and leave the controls to use your hands.'

He went on to take over the controls, and established a steady position. His pupil then took his hands and feet off the flight controls, letting the helicopter hover on its own.

'Sir! This is not a Cheetah. This aircraft is different. Remember, you are giving inputs to a logic-based system. You need to think and act accordingly.'

This was among the first of the many training instruction sorties Major Gulati flew with Lt Col Das, and other trainee pilots of the squadron, to make them fully 'operational' on the advanced helicopter—fully 'Ops on Type'—as known in the Army Aviation parlance. Army Aviation Squadrons consist of some truly underrated heroes. Their members are required to maintain the posts cut off from the rest due to snow and treacherous terrains in winters. There are times when the aviators have to leave at short notice, even in the middle of the night, because wounded soldiers keeping vigil on high mountain peaks may require immediate evacuation. Though they get to experience these glorious moments and save many lives, there are also occasions when the flight dispatcher on board informs them that a rescued soldier has breathed his last. Such moments can be excruciating, but even then, they cannot afford the luxury of mourning and are forced to remain dispassionate and continue operating to get the machine safely back on the ground.

In many ways Rajesh was training the next generation of pilots, who would go on to man these newly inducted state-of-the-art machines in the high-altitude battlefields of Kashmir, Ladakh, and the Siachen Glacier, not to forget the thickly forested hills in the North-east. The deployment of the ALH on these frontiers introduced an unprecedented operational capability in the Indian Army.

Col Sunil Kumar Das, who had worked closely with 'Lt Col Gulati' said to me, 'Rajesh was a pioneering member of our squadron, which trained for, and was the first to achieve, the Full Night Operations capability using Night Vision Goggles (NVGs) in the helicopter fleet of the Indian Defence Forces. In fact, he was a part of the crew that carried a jeep (Maruti Gypsy), underslung from the helicopter by night, and inducted a small team of Special Forces during an exercise in Rajasthan in 2009. This was the first time it had been done in the history of aviation in the country.'

Sometimes Destiny weaves a situation and introduces people in the most striking manner. The surreal encounters might be imprinted upon your mind forever. Col Sunil Kumar Das (now retd) held one such relationship with Rajesh. He was senior to Rajesh, but Rajesh was appointed as his instructor when they met in Nashik. Col Das was also with him during his last days at Manasbal, as his Commanding Officer.

* * *

2012
Dras

Major Rajesh Gulati had recently been promoted to the rank of Lieutenant Colonel, and had taken over as 2IC Second-in-command of 110 Medium Regiment, based at Dras. Surviving in high-altitude areas is tough. The terrain is rugged, the weather is cruel, and the uncertainty of life lingers amidst avalanches. We, living here in the cities, can never understand the pressure on the soldiers trying to keep pace with day-to-day life. They have to be physically fit, and also have to keep their morale high. Dras, especially, is a harsh posting even for the Indian soldiers famed for occupying the world's highest battlefields.

Lt Col Gulati personally took care of the overall physical and mental well-being of the troops under him, and pushed their limits in all dimensions—physical, mental, and spiritual. He aimed to reach out to the lowest of the ranks, and keep everybody's morale high. He would play cricket with them, go out patrolling with them, share rotis, and sometimes even cook the langar food for them himself.

Sarika and Saksham visited him during the holiday period. Dras being a field station, Sarika had had to stay behind in Jhansi. She said to me, 'Rajesh was excited and overjoyed. He did not even allow us to acclimatize to Leh, as was the protocol. We boarded his helicopter and reached his battalion at Dras in the blink of an eye. The place looked ethereal with its soaring snow-capped peaks disappearing into a burnt-orange sky. Some white mountains punctuated with little explosions of green took my breath away.

'I felt as if I had my own aviator from Pearl Harbour. My heart was filled with so much love. Saksham was excited too. We were put up in the Battalion Officers' Mess. In the mornings he would serve tea to me himself, and sometimes even arrange for pastries which, I must say, were a luxury at those heights. Sometimes he would ask me to pack some lunch, and we would spend that day at the banks of the beautiful Dras River near his office.'

Now that her husband is gone, those days feel like a mirage. Sometimes the memories don't allow her to sleep for days.

* * *

2012
Tangdhar Sector, Kupwara
Close to the LoC
North Kashmir

Col Sunil Kumar Das, Commanding Officer 202, Army Aviation Squadron, received a call in the middle of the night about a Gorkha battalion outpost upon the hills on the LoC having caught fire. The Pakistanis had broken the ceasefire once again, and were constantly firing across the LoC from their posts. They were striding towards the Leepa Valley in Pakistan-occupied-Kashmir, and heading for positions in India.

The enemy fire had hit the kerosene stock of the Gorkha battalion outpost, leading to a fire. Four soldiers were critically burnt and needed immediate evacuation.

There was a heavy exchange of fire between the Pakistani posts and their own. Col Das called Lt Col Rajesh Gulati, who was now one of his two Flight Commanders, and asked him to roll out the standby night aircraft they both would be flying to bring their injured soldiers over. He knew the sortie would be risky, and their own lives could be in danger. The helipad was located on a razor-sharp ridge line, and was under direct observation and fire by the enemy. They met at the aircraft upon dispersal, donned and adjusted the focus on their NVG helmets, and took off in their Dhruv helicopter.

Before the take-off, Lt Col Gulati had contacted the Commanding Officer of the Gorkha battalion over the telephone and assured him of their arrival. 'We are coming. Don't worry. We promise to evacuate the boys. Be ready with the casualties. The doors will be open. We'll have only a couple of minutes on the helipad before we take off again to avoid being hit by enemy fire. Be prepared.'

A helicopter for the troops at the forward posts has always been a symbol of hope. The incoming helicopter could see the arcs of fire between the two sides lighting up the night sky, while flying around the folds of the pitch-dark Valley.

One mistake, and they could add themselves to the list of casualties.

Rajesh was an excellent pilot. He used his knowledge of both the machine and the terrain, for cover. He also employed his superior skills gained from having spent hundreds of hours behind the controls. In an attempt to avoid collision with the mountains, he stealthily approached the helipad from below. They quickly landed on the helipad indicated by the torchlights, took the causalities on board, and dived back into the Valley. They managed to pull out of the Valley in a matter of a few minutes which, at that time, seemed agonizingly long.[20]

During our conversation Col Sunil Kumar Das laughed loudly, and said, 'It took some time before our heartbeats returned to normal, and we were able to climb to a safe altitude while flying back to BB Cantonment, Srinagar.'

Col Das also mentioned how their base was under the threat of terrorist attacks. 'The life near the LoC was full of risks. The terrain was tough, and we had intelligence reports of the enemy targeting many Air Force and aviation bases. Our squadron was one of the targeted bases. We took those inputs seriously, and slept with our weapons beside us. It was later in 2016 that the enemy succeeded in carrying out one such attack at the Pathankot Air Force station.'[21]

* * *

2014
Manasbal, Srinagar

The flood hit the Kashmir Valley following incessant rains. It was the worst flood recorded in the history of Kashmir. Not an inch of earth was visible. Houses, buildings, government offices, hospitals—everything was submerged under several feet of water. People were stuck on their terraces, and many prayed for help from the treetops. It was catastrophic. The Army stepped up the relief efforts.

Boats, rescue teams, and divers were deployed. The Air Force and the Army Aviation helicopters were also readied for action.

The ALH Squadron Flight Adjutant received a call about a capsized rescue boat belonging to the Army, and was told that the rescue team personnel were reported missing. The weather was still terrible; no air effort had yet been launched in the rescue ops. The entire Valley was covered with clouds, and the rains had not yet stopped.

Given the conditions, and the situation, Col Sunil Kumar Das and Lt Col Rajesh Gulati took off in their helicopter once again. It was the first aircraft to be airborne in the entire Kashmir Valley since the weather had turned bad. It was dangerous to fly, and to remain out of the clouds. To be able to see the ground, one was forced to fly low. Even then one could enter the clouds at treetop level. Hillsides, hillocks, high tension power lines with their pylons, mobile phone towers, and even the tall poplar groves, were an ever-present danger that could prove fatal if one ran into them inadvertently.

Both the pilots used the weather radar, the radio altimeter, the navigation equipment on board, and their knowledge of the lay of the land to reach the Jhelum and fly low over the waters—as they knew that other than the bridges, there would be no man-made obstructions on it.

Once again Col Das said to me, 'Rajesh, with his excellent piloting skills, kept the aircraft flying safely, navigating through all the hazards to reach the last known position of the rescue boat. Only skilled pilots could fly in such conditions. There was no sign of either the boat or the rescue team. We then flew downstream for a few kilometres, and found that they had somehow managed to climb onto the low overhanging branches of some trees at a bend in the river. Due to the obstructions around, it was challenging to attempt an aerial rescue. We did not want to risk the men losing their grip trying to board the aircraft, and falling into the Jhelum—flowing at a furious pace. They seemed safe for now. We noted their exact GPS coordinates and radioed them to our Air Traffic Control (ATC) to pass on to the HQ at Srinagar to coordinate a rescue over the ground.'

As the weather improved, Rajesh was at the forefront of the rescue effort, flying scores of the rescue-mission and aid sorties, pulling out hundreds of their own troops, as well as civilians, from the flooded posts and villages. He and his men also delivered food, medicines, blankets and other relief material to the stranded.

Sarika was always worried. During the floods she would hardly receive any calls from Rajesh. She was blissfully unaware of this superman of a husband, who was busy saving hundreds of lives. To her only his well-being mattered. She did not know he turned into a hero every time he flew his helicopter. Just like Batman in a mask saving Gotham.

Rajesh was about to complete his tenure in the field and return home soon, and the couple had several happy plans to which they looked forward.

* * *

11 February 2015
Manasbal
2.30 p.m.

Col Sunil Kumar Das, the CO, was briefing his Flight Commanders about the sorties to be flown that night. The Commanding Officer was entrusting his best pilots with the two-aircraft mission. Rajesh was to captain one of the aircraft with a young aviator, Major Tahir Hussain Khan, who was training to become 'Combat Ready on Type'.

'You know it will be dark. With greatly reduced in-flight visibility the terrain is hazardous, especially with the Safapura Ridgeline on the east. You will have to rely on all your instruments to navigate and remain clear of the obstructions. Remember to keep to 270 degrees, which is a westerly heading as your getaway direction,' he said.

Rajesh had just returned from an intensive three day-and-night exercise with the Special Forces (SF) that morning, where they had validated several SF tasks, including many by night, which involved extensive flying with NVGs. Towards the end of the exercise he had had the painful task of flying the mortal remains of a Special Forces operative to his native village in Himachal Pradesh. The soldier had, unfortunately, drowned in one of the amphibious training missions. Such sorties always took an emotional toll on them.

Besides, it had not been even fifteen days since Rajesh had flown the mortal remains of Col M.N. Rai, CO 42 Rashtriya Rifles, after he had attained martyrdom fighting against Hizbul terrorists in the Valley. Rajesh was also one among the many who had wept when Col Rai's eleven-year-old daughter, Alka, had raised the battalion war cry, 'Tiger 9GR, ho ki hoina?' [Tiger of 9 Gorkha Rifles, was he or not? The greatest of all, was he or wasn't he?] 'Ho, Ho, Ho!' [yes he was, he was] during his funeral. The video clip had been aired on national media, and widely circulated on social media.[22]

On 11 February 2015 two Dhruv helicopters, one being captained by Lt Col Rajesh Gulati, took off for their mission at 7.30 p.m. Just as the helicopters were starting up, Rajesh called up Sarika, and she could hear the whirring noise of the massive rotor blades in the background. This was the last time they spoke with each other.

The area domination patrols in Kashmir by the Forces, day and night, to flush out militants from their hideouts was routine. Helicopters were used to provide various types of tactical and logistical support to their own troops as they carried out their tasks. Col Gulati had been allotted one such important operation.

Major Tahir Hussain Khan, the passionate young aviator who was co-piloting with Rajesh, was keen on flying—and Rajesh always eager to teach. He handed over the controls to Tahir to enable him to gain experience and confidence in the use of instruments, to fly over hazardous terrain by night. In hindsight the instructor in Rajesh, and his willingness to pass on his skills to the younger pilot, got the better of him that fateful night. However, he knew they were close to the deadly Safapura Ridge, and even warned the young pilot that his indecisiveness over which way to turn might result in their crashing into the hill. He was late in taking over the controls from young Tahir by a few microseconds. They avoided the ridge in time but, as they moved away from the central hill, they collided with a spur jutting out from it.

The ATC could see a big ball of fire in the sky, and they knew something terrible had happened. The aircrew from the second helicopter radioed-in the occurrence. They returned to the base to take the Commanding Officer to the site of the crash. Upon reaching there, Col Sunil Kumar Das realized that the helicopter was burnt to the core. He knew nobody could have survived. It was an irreparable loss. They had just lost their most skilled pilot, Lt Col Rajesh Gulati.[23]

All ongoing ground operations were halted by the Rashtriya Rifles Commanding Officers in the area, and the troops on the ground were moved to the crash site as rescue parties. Rajesh was known to all the ground troops. They too were grief-stricken by the loss of such a dynamic pilot with a never say die attitude.

The young wife of Major Khan was in Manasbal at the time. They were newly-weds, not even a year into their marriage. She went into a deep state of shock, unwilling to believe what she had heard.

As Col Das was speaking to me, he paused for the longest time before he said with choked emotions, 'In the battle zone that most of the Kashmir Valley is, we are accustomed to seeing the loss of lives. However, when you lose one of your own, the hurt is deep and leaves you with an invisible scar. That remains long after you deinduct from an active zone or retire from military service. I had never thought that one day I would have to call Sarika to give her such terrible news. She had been expecting to hear from Rajesh, but received my call instead. Mrs Khan was inconsolable too. Tahir was a promising young aviator. We had high expectations from him, and that is why he was being exposed to Combat Flying at Night.'

* * *

11 February
Dwarka
9.00 p.m.

Sarika did not believe an ounce of what Col Das told her on the phone. Her Raj could not go like this. Col Das must be delusional, she thought. Fear clogged her soul. Perhaps she did know the truth, but did not want to acknowledge it. But once a group of aviation officers and their wives arrived at her house, she collapsed on the floor. Young Saksham suddenly turned mature and consoled his mother. 'Don't worry, Mamma. Nothing has happened. I am here. I will take care of you.'

He went on repeating this to the inconsolable Sarika, even during the last rites, when Sarika could hardly stand on her feet and fainted many times. The twelve-year-old turned into a man holding his mother like a rock. He did not cry once.

Everything happened in a blur after that. Sarika does not remember the details clearly. For around two years she had to be on antidepressants. She would not eat or sleep, and for days she would not cry—until her tears began to flow and would not stop.

Lt Col Rajesh Gulati was awarded the Sena Medal (gallantry) posthumously.[24]

* * *

The story is based on the interviews with Mrs Sarika Gulati, wife of Lt Col Rajesh Gulati; Col Sunil Kumar Das, his Commanding Officer; Col Mumkush Mehra, his course mate. When I met Sarika on 13 August 2019, during my second book launch, I found her looking sad. I could see the sadness even when she smiled. You can make out these things. The smile would never reach her eyes. They always looked welled up. There was no brightness on her face. She had still not been able to cope with her grief. Today she runs a LPG gas agency in Ghaziabad. She has named it 'Veer Raj Smriti HP Gas Service' in the loving memory of her soulmate. She looks forward to Saksham's visits. He studies in a boarding school now and frequently visits his mom.

An Empowered Woman

Jaya Mahto and
Lance Naik Raj Kumar Mahto

Dear Jaya,

I know you are not prepared for this. You don't want to marry, because you think I will not let you study, and you will end up working in the fields as a labourer—just like your elder sister. But, trust me, this is not my intention. My father has been forcing me to meet girls for marriage. For him, I am past the marriageable age already at twenty-three. After all, it is too late. But I haven't been able to fulfil his wishes because all the girls I met were uneducated, and I want an educated life partner so that she can raise my children right—and also step into the shoes of an Army wife conveniently.

Army relationships demand a lot of patience and persistence. My job is challenging. I am seldom at home. I want an educated life partner, who understands my job pressures, and supports my endeavours, while I support hers wholeheartedly. You see, it is essential for me to do my duties freely.

Marriages are destined. These relationships are indeed created in heaven, and I believe we are destined for each other. If you doubt I will allow you to study further, please take this letter as a Bond Paper. No matter what, I will always support your endeavours, and fulfil your dreams of further education. But I also want you to promise that you will never back out. Also, you should know that I am a duty-bound soldier. The moment I took part in 'Kasam Parade', my nation became my priority over everything else. She is my first mother; my own mother comes second. And, if you marry me and become my wife, you will be third on my list of priorities. If you think you can walk tall with me, I will marry you within fifteen days.

Yours truly,
Raj Kumar

* * *

April 1997
Tatisilwai, Ranchi
Jharkhand

Jaya was dumbfounded. The prospective groom, who had visited her house for the second time in a row for her hand in marriage, was nothing like the other men she had ever come across. Not only was his shirt neatly pressed, and the shoes shone unlike the other tribal men she had seen around, but he was also polite, well behaved, and progressive. He was certainly different.

Jaya Mahto was just sixteen when marriage proposals started flooding her house, as was the custom in their small tribal community, where girls were usually married off by thirteen and sometimes even earlier. Her father belonged to the Kurmi Mahto community in Jharkhand. He was a progressive man, who valued education. Jaya was his eldest child, and also the most studious. He put her in a private school—Carmel Convent—despite his financial constraints. He had no job; the factory he worked in had been shut down recently. Jaya had passed her tenth standard with good marks, and wanted to continue her education, but her father was going through a financial crisis. The humble man was also aware that Jaya was past the marriageable age in their community already. A few more years, and no one would marry his daughter.

The last time his daughter had not even appeared before the prospective groom. This time he could not allow her to dissuade Sepoy Raj Kumar Mahto. The family pressure on her to get married was immense, and her grandmother even suggested that she should be caged in a *khancha*—a huge bamboo container sealed with cow dung to make it airtight to store and preserve rice. She liked the short-haired, six-feet tall fauji a lot though. The only problem was dealing with her fears.

Jaya had seen her cousin being lured into marriage by her fiance´ with fake promises of literacy, only to be pushed into the fields to work as a labourer. She did not want a similar fate for herself. Raj Kumar seemed different. She was also under pressure, especially from the maternal side of her family. They had assured her that since the boy was in a government job, she would be well taken care of. After much thought, the sixteen-year-old nodded a yes, holding Raj Kumar's first letter firmly in her hand.

They were married within the next fifteen days (20 May 1997), as Raj Kumar had promised. There was singing, dancing, tribal food in earthen pots, and rice beer (handiya) to celebrate their union. As was the tradition, the whole village helped the bridal side during the wedding. The festivities continued for several days during the marriage rituals followed strictly by their tribe.

Eventually, Raj Kumar took her to his village, Masu. After she had stepped on bamboo-tokris lined with Sakhua leaves, she was welcomed into her new family. Clad in an orange saree, with some fake gold jewellery, Jaya sat uncomfortably on their flower-laden bed on their first night. Masu was soon going to be a part of her identity. She eagerly waited for Raj Kumar.

Beating wives, and pushing them into unpaid slavery, was usual for the men in their village. Her friends had told her that Army men were also aggressive and tamed their women from Day One.

When Raj Kumar entered the room, though she was excited she was also palpitating with fear. He sat down beside her feet, and asked her to remove the veil from her face. Then he said, 'Jaya, could you please give me that letter? I hope you brought it with you?'

Jaya was confused. This was the first time Raj Kumar was talking to her after their wedding. She nodded her head, and produced that letter after rummaging through her purse. Raj Kumar took it, and said, 'This is not only my first letter to you, but also an agreement between us. I am keeping it with me so that the moment you back out and decide not to study, I will show it to you. I want you to study well, because my job is risky. My wife must be self-sufficient not just to raise the children right, but also to face any situation boldly if I am no more.'

Jaya was shaken. Who could imagine talking about life and death on the first night of their married life? She said, 'How can you say such things? Nothing bad will ever happen to us. And, don't worry, I will work hard and make you proud. I will also help in the fields, but you'll have to ensure that my studies aren't interrupted.'

That was their first day together as a married couple, where they hoped for a better future. She had been married into a rural village, which was more backward than her own place, Tatisilwai, near Ranchi. There were no roads, and no hospitals or schools nearby. They didn't even have electricity. Water was fetched from a common village well. They lived in thatched huts, and farming was their primary source of livelihood.

Superstitions are still rampant in Jharkhand. In the nineties, they were like an epidemic, where women were branded as witches and lynched openly. No legal system ever helped them. The most progressive man in her life, Sepoy Raj Kumar, belonged there. He had braved all odds to carve a niche for himself. There were times when he had swum for hours to reach Government Middle School near Birla Institute of Technology, Mesra, in Ranchi. Life had never been easy for him, but now he was determined to further his wife's education.

He extended his leave for twenty more days, and spent around thirty days in all with his new bride. She had a wonderful time with her husband. The marital bliss lasted a month. Before leaving home, he informed everyone in the house that his wife had taken admission in the eleventh standard. He said, 'Pitaji, I have promised to support Jaya's education. She is a good student, and she passed her tenth standard with good marks. She has now taken admission in Ranchi Women's College, and I request you not to give her much work. Please support her studies while I am not here.'

His father was visibly upset, but it was his mother who spoke up. 'What are you saying? What will people say? You will not be here. What will our neighbours say if she goes around the place alone? Besides, who will work in the fields? We need more helping hands. We asked you to marry someone who had worked in the fields, but you married an educated girl, and now you want her to study further? It is not possible.'

Raj Kumar brought out some money, and gave it to his father. He said, 'Pitaji, I have already given her my word. Also, an educated mother will raise the children right. I am giving you money for a pakka ghar. Don't worry, I will give you extra money for her education as well.'

His parents kept quiet and nodded non-committally. Tribal communities are usually matrilineal societies. Sepoy Raj Kumar Mahto's mother, Jaimani Devi, was a dreaded figure in the house, and enjoyed complete command over her husband and sons. His elder brother, Amarnath Mahto, was totally mollycoddled. He had married at the age of ten and helped his father in the fields all through his life. His wife, Sita Devi, worked like a horse. The family members never wanted an educated daughter-in-law for their second son but, as he was the only proper earning member of the family, they could not disregard his wishes.

Raj Kumar Mahto left them to rejoin his unit 12 JAT, stationed at Binnaguri, West Bengal, at that time.

Subedar Major (Honorary Captain) Gopal Krishna Bhatt (retd) who was his senior in 12 JAT remembers him. During the interview he said, 'He was perhaps the most famous sepoy in the unit because of his football skills. He was an outfield player, a central defender—and prevented opposing teams from scoring goals, like a pro. He was swift, sharp, and sturdy. What impressed me the most were his leadership skills. He would focus on his game, and also encourage and motivate the entire team constantly. He used to say: "If you want to win, you have to work hard. If you cannot put sweat, blood, and tears in the game, forget about winning." It filled the players with new energy. We hardly ever lost a match with him in the team.'

One of his closest friends, Naib Subedar Zakir, who had fought in the Kargil War in 1999, said, 'He looked happy once he returned from his wedding, and shared sweets with everyone in the unit. He told everyone that his life partner, Jaya, was an intelligent woman. He also mentioned how he planned to educate her and make her a teacher.'

Lance Naik Raj Kumar Mahto, then a sepoy, was posted in 12 JAT Charlie Company's seventh platoon. An exuberant soldier, he was blessed with an agile mind and a sturdy body usual to tribal men from Jharkhand. Bubbling with infectious energy and vigour, he was a spirited man. No matter how many people I interviewed, they unanimously believed that he was a dynamic and passionate soldier—one who never said no to any work. He would be the one taking the initiative and going the extra mile to perform that task.

Naib Subedar Zakir remembers marching together with him during the Algara–Kalimpong war exercises, during the early months of 1998. He said, 'Those days were different times for the fauj. There were hardly any facilities or conveyances, and the emphasis was on strenuous physical activities. There were times when the battalions marched for twenty-four hours straight. We would only take little halts for food before we marched again. Raj Kumar would not rest even during those short breaks. While the other troops liked to sit, or take a nap, he would burn the stove to prepare tea for his comrades. That is how he was—always ready to help.' He also remembers the India–Bhutan joint Army exercises when they went to the Bhutanese town, Paro—a scenic little place surrounded with mountains.

Bhutan holds an important strategic position for India. At that time the nearly deployed 12 JAT was regularly involved with such joint military exercises with the Royal Bhutan Army.

He said, 'The devout Buddhist kingdom, ruled by a king, was a cultural surprise for us. The soldiers of the Royal Bhutan Army mainly used Sharchop and Dzongkha languages we did not understand. And they didn't understand any Indian languages. It would sometimes result in a laughter riot on either side, even though we had a translator during the training exercises.'

He paused for a moment before he said, 'I also remember him carrying the complete Medium Machine Gun (MMG) set on his back during those military exercises. The 7.6 mm MMG, along with its tripod, was quite bulky for a normal soldier, but Mahto disliked dismantling it. He would tell me to load it on his back and, when he felt tired, he would pass it to me.'

Zakir and Raj Kumar were great friends, and spent a good amount of time together until Raj Kumar was selected for the National Security Guard (NSG) unit, and left the glacier. The 12 JAT had moved to Siachen Glacier from Binnaguri, West Bengal, during late months of 1998. It was then that it recommended Sepoy Mahto's name for the NSG.

The National Security Guard (NSG) was set up in 1984 as a Federal Contingency Deployment Force to tackle all facets of terrorism in the country. It is one of the finest counter-terrorist units in the world, performing a variety of roles from counter-terrorism to hostage rescue, to VIP protection. A task-oriented force, modelled on the pattern of the Special Air Service (SAS) of the UK and GSG-9 of Germany, it has two complementary elements in the form of Special Action Group (SAG) and Special Ranger Groups (SRG). SAG, the offensive wing, comprises army personnel who are given different roles.

The selection process is one of the most robust among the Indian Armed Forces. Only the crème de la crème of various units, who usually excel in all the fields, are able to make it to the NSG. That was exactly why the CO 12 JAT recommended Sepoy Raj Kumar's name for the NSG.

* * *

Masu, Jharkhand

After Raj Kumar joined his unit, leaving behind the new bride, Jaya's mother-in-law made sure that she involved her in the household chores and the field work. Everything was new to Jaya. She had never worked in the fields, or with cattle. She and her sister-in-law, Sita Devi, would wake up at dawn, finish their household chores—which included cooking food for all the family members, separating rice from the chaff, cleaning utensils, sweeping the floors, preparing fodder for the cattle, and making cow dung upalas for fuel—before leaving for the fields where they worked as labourers. They would return home by evening, and immediately start cooking for the family, and finish the unfinished chores before the close of the day.

Jaya tried her best. When her parents had been told about the government job her husband had, nobody even expected this situation, but she carried on gracefully for the sake of her education. She knew if she refused to do the household chores, her in-laws would not allow her to study further.

Certain things troubled her, such as the issue of personal hygiene. Since water was not readily available, and had to be fetched from the village well, her mother-in-law would not allow them to bathe. She found it a waste of their time and resource, and abused her incessantly if she ever tried to wash. There was nothing odd about it. Older women in the village were expected to keep their daughters and daughters-in-law on a leash. Jaya had to bathe secretly at the village well, praying nobody would notice. She was not offered proper food either. Women in Masu were expected to feed only on leftovers. It was indeed a backward village.

Many of my readers may find it difficult to digest, but this treatment of women is still a reality in many parts of our country even today. Women are shackled in various chains, and the life of a jawan's wife—whose husband is far away—can be even tougher. Communicating with the husband was tough as there were no phones, and the letters reached once every month.

However, Jaya did not give up and attended her classes whenever she could. It was a promise she had made to her husband, and she did not intend to break it under any circumstances even when giving up would have been an easy option.

Raj Kumar visited Jaya in November 1997, just before the 12 JAT was to move to the Glacier from Binnaguri. Happier times knocked on her door again. Raj Kumar would help Jaya in almost everything. He would fetch water from the well, work in the fields, and make fodder for the cattle, along with his wife. He would also drop Jaya at the village bus stand, on his cycle, from where she took a bus to her college. This enraged his parents and they often taunted him for being a 'joru ka ghulam'. The villagers also mocked him for helping his wife, but it never deterred him. He was deeply committed to her. A woman was not a commodity to him. The progressive Army man knew manliness was proved on the battlefield through bravery, not at home by beating wives.

The night before leaving home he held Jaya's hand in his, and said, 'My friends back in unit taunt me that I'm obsessed with your education. They say I should keep you with me. Sometimes I also feel the same way, when I see you working so hard here. I know my mother does not treat you well. You don't deserve that, but you have to understand she is my mother. I can never go against her wishes.'

Jaya replied, 'I feel fortunate to have a life partner like you. What Ma says never matters, because I know you love me with all your heart. I also want to join you and, if you wish, I will give up my studies.'

Raj Kumar leapt up from their charpoy, and rummaged through his trunk. He produced the old letter and put it on Jaya's palms. He said, 'God knows how desperately I want to be with you, but this bond keeps my feet shackled. I obtained education with great difficulty. I want you to study because you are a fauji wife, and you should always be prepared for the worst. Your education will not only liberate you, but also make you self-sustaining. Most importantly, you will be able to differentiate between right and wrong and bring up our children properly.'

Jaya could not ask for more. She knew her husband wished the best for her. Raj Kumar left the next day, with his heart still with Jaya—who saw him off from across the bamboo door.

Jaya's sister-in-law, Sita Devi, died by suicide in December. Jaya was at college at that time, but this incident affected her deeply. Superstitions surrounded the rural Jharkhandi village. Apart from women branded as witches and lynched brutally, she had also seen children as young as five getting married, and people offering sacrifices to ghosts. She was determined to move away from all the social evils, and live in a better world—where she could groom her children well. Her brother-in-law, Amarnath Mahto, remarried in March.

Raj Kumar visited them in April again. It was also the time when she got pregnant with their first child, Gaurav, who was born in January 1998. After Raj Kumar left, there were times when she was asked to sell vegetables in the local haat, which she refused firmly. This was beneath her dignity. She said to her mother-in-law, 'I will do anything, but I cannot sell vegetables in the market. What if my parents or my neighbours see me? They will mock me. Even though I'm married to a government employee, I have to sell vegetables.'

She then shifted to her parents' place back in Tatisilwai for the rest of her pregnancy period. Once she needed Rs 1,200 for her class-twelve board-exam form, and there was no one who could lend her the money. She tried approaching her in-laws, but they refused even though her husband had given them a good amount of money for her care. She was too embarrassed to borrow money from her own parents, who were not financially stable themselves. The deadline to fill the form was approaching, and she was distraught. If she did not fill the form, her whole year would be wasted. She begged almost everyone she knew in Raj Kumar's circle— from friends to family, to relatives, but nobody came forward.

There was no way to inform Raj Kumar, as he and his team had moved to a forward post up in the Glacier, with no phone or connectivity. Finally, her distant uncle lent her the money and she could finally submit her exam form.

She said to me, 'I was heartbroken, but not broken. The world valued me when my husband was around but, in his absence, nobody came forward to help me even when I begged them—at the cost of my dignity. But that incident made me even more determined to complete my education and stand on my own feet. Though many times suicidal thoughts crept into my mind, I decided not to give in. Be it my pregnancy or my board exams, I silently promised the child in my belly that I would bring him/her into this world, no matter what—and that I would also pass the exams. After all, I was married to a fauji—and he had never taught me to give up.'

As the date of delivery approached, she was still in a dilemma. Private hospitals were out of her reach, and she had no money. One of her mother's neighbours told her about Military Hospitals, and she decided to go there. She had no 'Dependent' card or any identity proof. Raj Kumar always came for limited periods, and he had never had the opportunity to get her a 'Dependent' card. He had never felt any need for it either, since Jaya lived in Masu. Because of the lack of telephone services, no communication could be established with him.

When she reached the Military Hospital, she was asked for the 'Dependent' card. She was heavily pregnant, and her delivery was expected any time. Nobody wanted to take the responsibility without any identity proof. She did not even have a clear idea about her husband's unit. In frustration, she produced all the letters Raj Kumar had ever written to her. They came with the unit stamp. That was all the Military Hospital needed to confirm her identity. Like angels sent by the Gods, they helped her out against the standard protocols. She delivered a healthy baby boy in January 1998.

By then Raj Kumar's Company had moved back to the base, and he flew to Ranchi immediately to meet his newborn child. When he took the bundle of joy in his arms, he said, 'Jaya, I always thought I was the soldier, but it is you who fought the war. If you could deliver this boy in the Military Hospital despite the problems, I am sure you can handle anything in my absence now.'

Jaya smiled feebly before closing her eyes in relief. Raj Kumar was there for the next twenty days. While he was there, Jaya also appeared for her class-twelve board exams. Raj Kumar looked after the newborn until she returned home. Then she held the baby in her arms and fed him. It was a draining time for her physicaly and mentally, but she did not give up. She knew she only had one chance.

After Raj Kumar left, Jaya moved back to Masu. She had been at her mother's place for the past several months and, now that her exams were over, she thought she could move back to her sasural after her admission in a graduation college. She had opted for BSc Zoology Hons in Ranchi Women's College.

Holding the baby in her lap, she would do all the household chores and also work in the fields. She would not let that affect her studies. She would study in whatever little time she had, sometimes in the fields, sometimes in the kitchen, and sometimes while feeding her baby—who made her forget all the hardships she had endured.

Meanwhile, Lance Naik Mahto had been selected for the NSG. His first posting was to Samlakha, Delhi, in 52 SAG, the anti-hijacking squad. From leading an infantryman's life to leaping to the NSG wing was a massive achievement for Raj Kumar. His salary increased, and so did his living standards.

* * *

1998
Manesar

Raj Kumar was an excellent footballer and a runner. That helped him clear the complex selection process of the National Security Guards (NSG). It is an elite special response force, raised in 1986, to fight against terrorism and protect the Indian states against any internal disturbance—such as an aeroplane hijack or a hostage situation. It is involved in the rescue operations, and takes care of VIP protection and other special operations. The training-and-selction process is extremly tough and demands zero error. The soldiers that make it to the list need to be physically robust and mentally agile. They also need to have excellent records of high integrity and commitment to duty from their past units. Here, Raj Kumar's exceptional sportsmanship, and his devotion to duty, played an important role in his selection.

Sepoy Raj Kumar's basic training began at the National Security Guard Training centre, Manesar, Haryana. His week comprised various physically and mentally challenging tasks—from intense running within an impossibly short time on some days, to the Battle Proficiency Efficiency Test (BPET)—when he ran several kilometres with heavy load on his back—in full NSG gear, to the Physical Proficiency Test (PPT) on other days.

Twice a week he would also perform the Herculean Battle Obstacle Course (BOC), and cross twenty-six types of obstacle. From jumping from great heights to dangling from a rope, to crawling under barbed wires in the mud—there was nothing he did not perform—and always came out as excellent. His sportsman skills came in handy during his training. The Black Cat Commandos are considerd the best snipers in the country, and special emphasis is put on making them excellent marksmen. Raj Kumar and his peers practised firing at short and long ranges almost every day for hours, aside from taking physical tests. When Raj Kumar was not firing, he learnt Karate and unarmed combat skills. It was a rigorous schedule.

Raj Kumar did exceptionally well at his basic training, and was selected for advanced training—unlike many of his peers, who were sent back home after the first leg. The advanced training familiarized him with various sophisticated weapons and equipment. He learnt to assemble, dismantle, and use weapons like the MP 5 rifle, the high-power 9 mm pistol, the MP-5 SD (silencer device), and others. Since he was marked for the 52 Special Action Group (SAG), which dealt with anti-hijacking operations, during the advanced training he was taught about almost every aeroplane in the world—their structure, construction, emergency doors, and other features. The night-time drills at various airports thrilled him—when he, along with his 'hit'—barged through the aeroplane doors to rescue imaginary hostages. Then they would be asked to shoot the dummy terrorists using only one bullet. Raj Kumar was a good shooter, but the NSG training transformed him into an excellent one.

His skills were why the Indian Army utilized him for high-risk field jobs at critical places once he finished his tenure at the NSG. After the NSG, he was posted to the 5 Rashtriya Rifles located at Ganderbal, Kashmir—where he attained veergati.

Once his advanced training was finished, Sepoy Raj Kumar was posted to the 52 SAG Cheeta group, an anti-hijacking unit. The members were deployed across the Indian airports in civil uniforms as invisible Forces, who would act only if exceptional situations arose. Their involvement was more around the airports bordering Pakistan. The NSG tenure was a great time for him and his wife as a couple, because now he got leave almost every three months, and was often at home. If he was en route to Ranchi, then too he showed up for a day to meet his family.

During his NSG tenure in 1999–2002, Jaya got pregnant with their second child, Ankit. She was not sure about her second pregnancy, but Raj Kumar said, 'Jaya, my job is risky and my life is always at stake. The children will be your ray of hope if something happens to me. You must not think twice about our second child. Let him/her come.'

Jaya said to me, 'I was furious with him, and scolded him. Why did always he bring life and death into our conversation? But now I think he was always preparing me for the worst. He had some kind of premonition, perhaps. I read his letters now and realize they hinted at the worst, and reminded me of my role if it happened. I could have crumbled without his instructions. I felt I had lost everything in life, and also my zeal to move forward. His words in my subconscious showed me the path.'

When Gaurav was two years old, and Ankit three months, Raj Kumar got a proper accommodation in Delhi. He called his wife over to stay with him for a few months. She remembers how he would wear black dungarees, cover his face with a black mask, and also don a bulletproof vest and DMS boots. He carried a Heckler and Koch MP5-K operational briefcase, which contained the deadly gun inside it. Besides, there were NVGs with standard frames, chloroform in perfume bottles, advanced guns, and other things. The commando belt holster would adorn his body twenty-four hours a day, seven days a week. He would always be prepared. Jaya could not suppress her astonishment, and asked him about it.

He laughed and said, 'We at the NSG are always prepared for the worst. Tragedy can strike any time. At such times, between life and death, every single second counts. We are the last line of defence for our citizens; we cannot waste time getting ready when such a thing happens. Even during the training, we were firmly briefed about our code of conduct. So . . . whether you like your husband or not, you have to bear with him.'

Such men are the quintessence of all things glorious. Lance Naik Mahto was one of those souls. How I wish this fact could console Jaya. Can she ever come to terms with her loss? For her, he was not just a hero but also her husband, life partner, companion, and her children's father—with whom she had hoped to have the future they had always planned. She remembered the numerous letters where he had discussed their life once he got a peace posting.

In one of the letters he had specifically said, 'We will keep Ma with us, Jaya. Let me know. I will apply for a family accommodation, but I owe her a good life. Masu has enveloped her with bitterness. She has seen nothing but hardships. I am sure as soon as she starts living with us, the rancour in her heart will dissolve. After all, our children deserve their grandparents.'

They had made plans. They were working hard. The period from 1999–2002 was also the time when the NSG underwent significant reforms after the Kandhar hijack and the Parliament attack. Raj Kumar's role, too, evolved—and he started flying in disguise in passenger flights to ensure the safety of the passengers. He would put on make-up, bright clothes, goggles, a tie, and a coat or blazer, etc., to hide his identity as a commando.

During the Parliament attack, he was also a part of the operations. After completing a three-year stint with the NSG, he returned to his unit—the 12 JAT—which was in Jaipur that time. However, because of his skills, he was deputed into the 5 Rashtriya Rifles within five months.

(The NSG is a covert organization. Even though I wish I could reveal his active involvement in the various operations, I cannot—for the sake of confidentiality. But, true to his name, Raj Kumar was a prince who never hesitated to take heroic steps when it came to his nation and his people.)

* * *

The 5 Rashtriya Rifles
Ganderbal, Srinagar
Kashmir

Since the day Sepoy Rajuram (now serving as a Naib Subedar) had joined the 12 JAT, he had heard heroic stories about Lance Naik Mahto. His seniors would not stop citing examples of his courage, valour, and hard work, to the recruits. Young Raju had just been attached to the 5 Rashtriya Rifles located in Ganderbal, Kashmir, where Lance Naik Raj Kumar Mahto too was posted. Raju hoped to meet him soon. He would nervously check his boots, belt, and uniform, repeatedly on his way to the unit.

When he reached the base, and started unloading his trunk, a loud voice called out, 'Sepoy Rajuram?' Startled, he turned around to give a crisp salute to the senior standing before him. '*Ram Ram Sir! Sipahi Raju, 12 JAT, upasthit hai!* [Good morning, Sir. Sepoy Raju from the 12 JAT is here.]'

'*Oye! Teri to abhi muche bhi nahi aayi hai! Idhar 5 RR me kya kar raha hai?* [Hey, you don't even have any moustaches sprouting yet. What are you doing here]?' Lance Naik Mahto smiled generously.

'*Aapke bare me bahut kuch suna hai, aaj aapse mil bhi liya.* [I've heard a lot about you. Today I finally got to meet you too],' an overwhelmed Raju stammered.

'*Arrey! Ye unit wale bhi na aise hi hawa banate rahte hai. Chal itna load na le! Paani pi!* [Oh, these unit guys exaggerate everything. Don't stress yourself out. Have some water.]' Lance Naik Mahto patted his back affectionately.

Raj Kumar asked him to meet him the next day after duty, and also told him to approach him before anyone else if he faced any problem. After all they were from the same unit, and this was the most special bond the soldiers shared in the Indian Army.

The next day Sepoy Rajuram met him in the barracks, and said, 'Sir, you are my senior, and you have also been a commando, but this is my first posting of this kind. I am flummoxed. *Yaha to bhaut encounter hoti hogi*? [There must be many encounters here?]'

Lance Naik Mahto replied, 'This is what you have to learn in the RR. Our main job is not to engage in counter-terrorism operations or cordon-and-search. Our primary job is to maintain peace and brotherhood with the locals, and provide them assistance. CO Sahib meets all the village elders twice in a month to listen to their problems and provide support. The villagers put so much trust in us that they call for help with vehicles, medicines, and many other things. Many times I have put bandages on their wounds, or transported sick cattle to the nearest hospital. This is what we do here.' He paused for a moment and said, '*Tere ko ye nahi sochna ki wo* Hindu *hai ya* Muslim. *Bus itana yaad rakhna hai ki wo* Indian *hai aur tujhe unki har sahayata karni hai. Yahi humara kaam hai. Agar bahar wale humari dharti par kadam rakhnge, ya koi hum pe* bomb *phenkenge, to hum to jawab denge hi na. Isse* encounter *bolo ya kuch aur.* [Don't think whether someone is a Hindu or a Muslim. Just remember they are Indians and we have to help them. That's our job. If terrorists trespass on our land, or throw bombs at us, we'll retaliate, won't we? You can call it encounter or whatever.] '

Lance Naik Mahto also briefed him about their modus operandi and the safety measures they took where they operated. Kashmir at the time was infested with terrorism and categorized as a 'disturbed area'. Hence the Armed Forces Special Powers Act (AFSPA) is implemented there even today.

Raj Kumar explained to Rajuram that the prime contribution of the Rashtriya Rifles was not simply to neutralize the terrorists, but to maintain peace and stability in the area. He also told him how the RR worked in close association with the police. Their main job was to ensure a favourable situation for smooth civil governance. He also mentioned how he personally found working with Rashtriya Rifles more challenging than being a commando with the NSG. He emphasized on the roles of 'ikhwanis' or brotherhoods for gathering intelligence reports.

Sepoy Rajuram was awestruck by how much he knew, and what an incredible soldier he was. Comrades back in the unit were not wrong. Later that night, many soldiers met him and told him that Lance Naik Mahto was a buddy of the Company Commander because he was one of the best. The Rashtriya Rifles were not affiliated to separate regiments. The troops belonged to various arms and units.

Young Raju felt extremely proud to belong to the same unit—the 12 JAT—as Lance Naik Mahto. He didn't know that by strange coincidence, the lines on his palms were very similar to the ones on Raj Kumar's. Life is mysterious and certain things are still beyond human comprehension. There are questions with no answers, and there are things no science can explain. Rajuram was to witness one such thing.

During my interview sessions with Naib Subedar Rajuram, he said, 'I am back to my unit—the 12 JAT now and, whenever I cross our sports complex named after him, I am not able to control my tears. I was awestruck at his bravery and idolized him, as a young soldier, but I never knew then that I was destined to be with him during his last days. Sometimes I feel I was posted to the 5 Rashtriya Rifles only to meet him. Soon after I did, I was posted out to the 15 Corps QRT. That brief period in the 5 RR was like a halt for me. Maybe there was a past-life connection. I don't know.'

In that brief time during his attachment with the 5 RR, Sepoy Rajuram visited op areas with Raj Kumar, and accompanied him during 'Sadbhavna Missions.' The 5 Rashtriya Rifles provided security to a local school, and also looked after repair works. Sometimes, they would even pay the teachers to come and teach the local kids. There were times when Rajuram would perform night duties along with Raj Kumar.

Once Raj Kumar took him to meet a Kashmiri Pandit. Young Raju was getting acquainted with the Valley, and sometimes it took a toll on the soldiers. The gunfire, the violence, and sometimes the sheer display of brutality disturbed his mind. The security of the Kashmiri Pandit they met was the joint responsibility of the CRPF and the 5 RR. The Pandit counselled Raju. He narrated his own story about the time of the exodus of the Kashmiri Pandits from the Valley back in the 1990s.

Even though I persisted, Naib Subedar Rajuram refused to share the story. He said firmly, 'I cannot. His experience was beyond brutal. He had a family—sons, daughters, a wife, cousins—and now no one survives. It was a ghastly story—one that still haunts me. I don't want to unleash the demons again.' As if he was speaking to himself, he said, 'But he gave me much courage. He even performed a little pooja for me. I realized the repercussions in case the Army failed, and why I could not afford to be emotional or distracted.' He was lost in thought when he said, 'The Pandit also told me he was not afraid of terrorists any more. This was his land—the land of his forefathers—and he intended to perish on it. The terrorists had already snatched away everything that once belonged to him. I don't even know if he is alive or not now. Then Raj Kumar Sir also told us about his narrow escapes from death, and how nothing scared him any more because he believed that even if he died he would die for a noble cause. What a glorious way to go.'

That was the last conversation between the comrades. Soon after Rajuram was ordered to move to the 15 Corps, where he would be a part of the QRT for the rest of his tenure.

* * *

4 June 2004
Tatisilwai, Jharkhand

Jaya was in the final year of her post-graduation. Her final exams were due in November and she was working hard. A lot had happened over the past two years. Her courage and conviction had finally earned her the respect and support of her in-laws. The entire village turned up to congratulate her in-laws when she graduated with a first division in Zoology Hons in 2002. She was the first woman graduate from Masu, and she made headlines in the local newspapers for her extraordinary feat. Her father-in-law felt quite proud of her achievement in a village where women were shackled, and women's empowerment was a myth. This time he went with her when she went to fill the form for her MSc. He also instructed his wife not to burden Jaya with too much work, so that she could focus on her studies. The two boys already kept Jaimani Devi busy.

For once, when Jaya felt everything was under control, her father-in-law passed away in 2003. Things suddenly turned sour. People started calling Jaimani Devi a witch. It was not an uncommon treatment meted out to widows in that village. People would trouble Jaimani Devi a lot. Even today, in many parts of Jharkhand, people still believe in witchcraft and lynch women openly.[25] Twenty years ago the situation was even worse. Raj Kumar visited home thrice that year and threatened the villagers with an FIR if they made mischief. Things were normal as long as he was home. As soon as he left, people started troubling Jaimani Devi again. Jaya tried her best to educate them, but in vain.

But she was hopeful, and she waited for her husband to return home once again. Raj Kumar was about to complete his tenure with the 5 Rashtriya Rifles, and was planning to visit them on 7 June 2004, for a week. Jaya, too, was about to complete MSc, and she was not going to leave any stone unturned for a first division. They had plans to shift to Jaipur along with Jaimani Devi—where Jaya thought of completing her PhD. The 12 JAT had moved to a peace station in Jaipur. It would be great for the boys' schooling. Raj Kumar also promised to take her to Deegha—a beach town in West Bengal—as soon as he was home. Gaurav and Ankit, who were now five and two-and-a-half, had already sent a massive list of toys they wanted, in a letter to Raj Kumar. It also included a real tank. Jaya was counting every single second.

She clearly remembers the morning of 4 June 2004. She received a call from Lance Naik Mahto.

'Hello.'

'*Ram Ram Gaurav ki Mummy. Kaisi hai aap?* [Good morning, Gaurav's mum. How are you?]' The voice on the other side of the phone sounded happy.

'*Aaj phone kaise kar diya aapne itani subah subah? Aise to kabhi karte nahi ho aap?* [How come you rang so early in the morning today? You usually never do.]'

'*Arrey Gaurav ki Mummy, ab apne milan ke din aane wale hai. Aa raha hu 7 June ko. Socha surprise du isliye phone kiya. Raat se hi yaad bahut aa rahi hai aapki, pata nahi kyu. Isliye maine aaj rasgulle bhi khaye.* [Gaurav's mum, now the days for our reunion are coming. I'm coming on 7 June. I thought I'd give you a surprise so I called. I've been missing you a lot since last night, I don't know why. That's why I even had rasgullas today.'

'*Arrey*, how you could eat rasgulle? Those are my favourite sweets, and you hate them.' Jaya blushed.

'I told you—I am missing you a lot. It feels as if 7 June is an eternity away, and it will never come. I cannot wait to meet you and the kids,' an emotional Raj Kumar replied slowly.

'Please don't say that. It is just two days away, and they will evaporate in no time. How long will you stay this time?'

'I will be in Masu only for a week, take you people to Deegha, and leave for my unit immediately. But when I return, I will return as Naik Raj Kumar Mahto. Jaya, your husband will be a Naik now. My promotion is due in June. But I promise to return as soon as I am promoted,' Raj Kumar said with pride in his voice.

Jaya was thrilled. She knew what this promotion meant to him.

'*Accha, jaldi batao*, how is Ma? I have to go to Company Commander Saheb. He has asked me to meet him immediately, but I thought of calling you first.'

'Ma is fine, though the villagers are still harassing her. I am in Tatisilwai with my mother for a while, but I will return to Masu with you on 7 June when you come. Why has Sahib called you?'.

'Jaya, you have to be with her. After Papa passed away, she feels lonely. This time we will plan our move to Jaipur.

Ma needs a better life, away from all these nasty villagers. I will talk to CO Sahib about it once I reach the 12 JAT. Now I need to go. Take care. Bye. Love you.'

Jaya put down the receiver of the landline happily at her uncle's house. It was the last call from her husband before he made the supreme sacrifice within a few hours, while performing duties under 'Operation Rakshak'.

I wish we had a way of foreseeing our future so as to plan things better. Otherwise broken dreams, unfulfilled promises, and lost hopes, are what our soldiers leave behind for their families who mourn their untimely demise lifelong.

* * *

4 June 2004
Ganderbal
Kashmir

The Commanding Officer of the 5 Rashtriya Rifles was worried over the infiltration reports from across the border through Malutgali, Ganderbal. The terrorists were using Malutgali regularly to infiltrate the area, which fell under his domain. The Malutgali hill, and the nallah at its feet, proved to be an easy escape for the terrorists. The terrain was proving to be an enemy of the Forces, and they had to set up a post on the hill to monitor terrorist movement. Insurgency in Kashmir was at its peak during the early 2000s, and they were having a tough time dealing with it.

Such tasks are carried out under Operation Rakshak, which imposes much restraint on the Forces, and hinders their movement. Many security personnel have lost their lives to save local lives and, sometimes, for the sake of goodwill.

On 4 June 2004, they received reliable intel about two Lashkar terrorists hiding in Malutgali. The 5 Rashtriya Rifles QRT, including thirteen soldiers along with the Company Commander, left for the place. Lance Naik Mahto was a part of that QRT, because he was one of the best and also a friend of the Company Commander. He always worked in tandem with him. They were brothers-in-arms.

The cordon-and-search operation led them to realize that the terrorists were hiding on the dock. When they reached there, the terrorists were not in sight. Perhaps somebody had informed them about the movement of the Forces in the area. The Company Commander laid a trap, and the squad moved stealthily to take position all around the place. It was decided that Lance Naik Mahto would go ahead first, and Company Commander would provide him cover. They were banking on the element of surprise, without realizing that the LeT men had already acquired relatively safer positions. LeT boasted an excellent intelligence network in the valley. The terrorists had realized they could not break the cordon and escape, so they had decided to wait and fight to death.

The moment Lance Naik Mahto stepped forward to take his position, the first rounds were fired for less than sixty seconds. Taking position is naturally the most critical part of any operation, because then you are relatively safer. He was hit by several bullets and fell immediately.

One second! All it took was one second for things to turn upside down. The sturdy and experienced Lance Naik Mahto was the strength of his QRT—and also their moral support. Even the Company Commander could not stop himself from coming out of his cover, defying the protocol at such a time. He rushed towards the slain hero with two other soldiers. The rest of the 5 RR squad tightened their hold on the handles of their machine guns, and rained down multiple rounds of bullets upon the terrorists. It was only a matter of luck that the terrorists had the huge Malutgali nallah just beside them—into which they jumped to save their lives.

The two terrorists were eventually gunned down the next day by the 24 RR located in Kupwara. The 5 RR and the 24 RR had a lot of common op areas between their bases in Ganderbal and Kupwara.

Srinagar was around twenty-five kilometres away from the encounter site. Immediately, Lance Naik Mahto was moved to an ambulance towards the 92 base hospital in Srinagar. But the tough soldier succumbed to the multiple bullet shots on the way.

Sepoy Rajuram, from the same corps, rushed to the hospital once he got the news. He found the CO 5 Rashtriya Rifles, the Company Commander, and the senior JCOs there. They all looked devastated. Lance Naik Mahto had not been any ordinary soldier, but a commando. It was a huge jolt to their morale. The Commanding Officer moved towards Sepoy Rajuram once he saw him. He knew both of them were from the same unit.

Naib Subedar Rajuram said to me, 'He told me whatever had to happen had happened, and I shouldn't let it affect my morale, etcetera, but it felt as if he was consoling himself. We all knew what had been lost in our fight against terrorism. It was a miserable sight. I could not bear the thought of Jaya Bhabhi. I knew what he had done for her, and that he had just been about to complete his tenure and return home.'

The body was sent off to Ranchi. Jaya's brother-in-law, Amarnath Mahto, was the first one to receive the information. He hurried over to Jaya's parents' place where she was staying. Nobody told her anything, but she could sense something was wrong. Then she was told that Raj Kumar had been hit by bullets, and was injured, but it was nothing serious. But there was instinctive trepidation in her heart. She had been a strong tribal woman, the one who could carry all the burdens of this world on her shoulder, but this was something that made her shudder. She kept telling herself nothing could go wrong, and her husband would return home within two days as he had promised.

By late evening a huge crowd had gathered at her parents' house. People had come to know about the supreme sacrifice the 'local man' had made.[26] Jaya was in denial until she saw the body herself. Lance Naik Raj Kumar Mahto was wrapped in a Tiranga. She fainted. When she came round, she realized she had lost everything.

She said to me, 'I first thought about my children. Then I thought about myself. I was very young at that time—around twenty-one. It was because of his support that I could study, and I had been hoping for a good future for my children. I did not know who would help us now, and how we would survive without him. He had been my guiding light, my mentor and friend. Life suddenly felt meaningless.'

Jaya lost the will to live. Her children would howl with hunger, and she would not listen to them. She started having nightmares, and many times she would get up shivering in the middle of the night. She had no money, no support, and she did not know how long she could live at her parents' place. Her in-laws' home only meant the end of the dreams she had dreamt with Raj Kumar. She could neither educate herself nor her children.

God sends us angels in the form of people when we desperately need them. These angels can be our friends, family, or even strangers who appear for a brief while, bringing us strength and consolation, and fill our hearts with love. They deliver the message from God, and give us a sign—a hint—that not all is lost and He's watching over us. All we need to do is take the hint, have faith, and move on.

Jaya had her angel in Lance Naik L.B. Rai, who had worked with her husband at the NSG. He had travelled to Masu to meet the bereaved wife of his beloved friend once he heard the news. He said, 'Why did Raj Kumar educate you so well? To cry and grieve? Or to use that education when the time came? That time has come. Use it. Go through all the condolence letters, and see where you can find help.'

Jaya took out all the condolence letters. Out of them one letter from the President of the Army Wives Welfare Association (AWWA) caught her eye. The words 'Army Wives Welfare Association' printed on the letter hinted that this might be the right platform for her to put forward her grievances. She replied to that letter and received a message within a few days. The then-President of the AWWA, Mrs Rita Vij, guided her on further course of action. Then Jaya met the Chairperson of the AWWA 23 Infantry Division, Mrs Renu Bhardwaj, based in Ranchi, which was their local chain of command. Mrs Renu Bhardwaj, aware of her status as a veer nari, immediately sent a vehicle and asked her to meet her at her office.

Mrs Renu Bhardwaj, wife of Lt Gen. Dalip Bhardwaj— who was then General Officer Commanding, 23 Infantry Division, now retired—remembers the time. She said, 'Jaya was angry and distraught. It had been a month since I met her, and she felt that the Army had not helped her. I understood her pain. The Army is one big family, and these are our daughters. If we do not help them, who will?'

The first thing Mrs Bhardwaj asked her to do was to learn driving, which was revolutionary for someone who belonged to a backward village. She had hindrances, but Mrs Bhardwaj told her she would help her only if she helped herself first. For that, she needed to learn to drive a scooter. Mrs Bhardwaj also arranged for a scooter from the CSD and requested the concerned authorities to clear Jaya's finances. Jaya was also offered a job at the Army Public School, even when she was not qualified for the post. Mrs Bhardwaj said, 'The idea was to keep her engaged and provide her with a purpose. She was not willing to appear for her final exams in August either. I counselled her, and she agreed to do it. That turned out to be a milestone in her career.'

During that time Lt Gen. Dalip Bhardwaj organized an ex-serviceman rally for three days. Renu Bhardwaj insisted that he organize a veer nari rally for a day in between that rally.[27] As the Chairperson of the AWWA of that area, she met the veer naris at least twice a month, and she knew how they needed the system's support to move on—through the broken corridors of their lives. Renu Bhardwaj, as the wife of an armoured officer, had seen it all. She knew what it was like to lose a husband, or a father, and how traumatic it could be for the Army families.

To me she said, 'During my tenure, I ensured that I met the veer naris and the wives whose husbands were posted at the borders, at least twice a month. The Commanding Officers of the respective units would arrange for the vehicles, and the families would visit me at my office. That also made me aware of the problems the local women faced. So I insisted that my husband hold a veer nari rally. We invited bankers, builders, employment firms, social activists, ministers, and many more people.' The then Chief Minister, Sri Arjun Munda, readily agreed to facilitate this rally simply over a phone call from her.

The veer naris, including Jaya Mahto, were given Rs 200,000 at the function. Many applied for houses; many wanted admissions for their children—and several other things. All their official documents were corrected and compiled. They were helped in every way possible. Renu Bhardwaj also requested a known builder to provide a flat to Jaya on discounted rates. Added to it she arranged for a bank loan, and helped her with a fixed deposit for the money she had received after her husband's demise. She also told Jaya firmly to use it for her children's education and her own survival. Mrs Bhardwaj knew it was going to be tough for the young tribal woman to survive without the husband, and money was essential for that.

The builder agreed to give a flat for Rs 5,00,000 at that time, and waived off another Rs 1,00,000 after Renu Bhardwaj intervened. She said to me later, 'Swapnil, during the veer nari rally the builder agreed to it, and we started the process at once, but I remember Jaya calling me after we were posted to Delhi. She said that he hadn't handed over the flat and was delaying it constantly. I knew the Inspector General of the state, so I called him and requested his help. He called the builder. After that the builder called Jaya and said that she was like a sister to him. He promised to hand over the flat within a week –and he kept his promise.'

A vivacious giggle followed this. I smiled in return.

Jaya also remembers that time. She said, 'I feel so grateful to the Army for everything I have today. My husband was gone, but he left the whole Army fraternity for me. It's been fifteen years since he went, but the AWWA has always come forward to help me. I remember after my husband's veergati, the villagers in Masu started targeting me, too, and branded me as a witch. Three deaths in a row in the same house made everyone believe the theory. One day one of the known people informed me that villagers might try to lynch me as well as grab our lands. I was scared. In desperation I called Renu Ma'am and briefed her about my situation. The next morning I found the whole convoy of military vehicles in my village. The whole village was dumbfounded. The Subedar Major Sahib, who was leading the convoy, came to our thatched hut and with great respect escorted me out to our village chaupal.

'Around five soldiers walked behind me and others surrounded the area. They gathered everyone in the village, and announced that if anybody tried to hurt me or my family, the entire village would be sent off to Tihar Jail. This was also a hidden threat to them because they knew they could not come back from Tihar. That was the last day of my miseries. Everybody knew then that even if my husband was not there, I was not alone.'

The sentence ended with a peal of laughter, filled with hope and gratitude. The journey ahead was tough, but she did not give up on her dream to empower herself and become self-sustaining. She shifted to her own house in Ranchi as soon as she received the keys, and her dependence on other people ended. She was free to make her own decisions and move ahead in her life. After her MSc she also pursued BEd and MEd, while teaching at Army Public School. Later, she was offered a job by the Jharkhand government in 2016, after eleven long years of waiting as ex gratia. Her first posting was as a Science teacher in Dhanbad. She also taught as a lecturer at teacher-training programmes. In 2019, she was included in the ambitious e-learning programme of the Jharkhand Council of Educational Research and Training as an e-content developer.

From being a rural tribal woman to becoming a teacher, and spreading the light of education to young souls, Jaya has only emanated strength and courage. In that sense she has lived up to her name—one of the many Goddess Durga is known by. Jaya did not perish, or hide behind the closed doors of poverty and social stigma. Instead, she fought her way up the ladder, and has become a beacon of hope for hundreds of women like her. But then, this is what we expect from a woman married to a brave soldier—an Army wife.

Today Jaya is well settled. She not only has an MSc in Zoology and an MEd, but is also a TGT Science teacher in a government school in Jharkhand. She takes immense pride in fulfilling her husband's dream. Her elder son, Gaurav, after completing his BTech, Electrical Engineering, has just been placed at Tata Consultancy Services (TCS); and the younger son, Ankit, is in second year, pursuing Bachelor of Computer Application (BCA). She still lives in the same flat Mrs Renu Bhardwaj helped her buy, and remembers her husband every day after the national anthem at her school assembly.

* * *

The story is based on the interviews with Jaya Mahto, wife of Lance Naik Raj Kumar Mahto; Naib Subedar Zakir, who served with Lance Naik Mahto; Naib Subedar Rajuram, Lance Naik Mahto's junior, who served with him for some time; Honorary Captain Gopal Krishna Bhatt, his senior and football friend; and Mrs Renu Bhardwaj, the then Chairperson the AWWA of the 23 Infantry Division. Today, Masu has a bust of Brave Heart Lance Naik Raj Kumar Mahto, and a football tournament and a marathon are organized in his name every alternate year. Jaya also helps veer naris belonging to rural Jharkhand villages, the way the Army helped her. She counsels the girls of her area to be educated, and plans to open a library in Masu soon. She was also invited for the Golden Jubilee celebrations of the 12th battalion of the JAT Regiment on 6 February 2020—her husband's parental unit, which has not forgotten her even today. She has been the sole driving force in completing the long lost story of her husband. She helped me immensely in finding facts, researching, and connecting with the right people—all because she is adamant about keeping the legacy of her husband alive.

The Kargil Love Story

Sowmya Nagappa and Captain Naveen Nagappa, Sena Medal (Gallantry)

6 July 1999
Point 4875 (Now known as Batra Top)
Mushkoh Valley, Dras Sector

Dawn was about to break over the steep slopes of the treacherous Point 4875,[28] a crucial and strategic mountain top for the Indians and their Pakistani enemies. These were the barren lands: no trees, no bushes, just snow-capped mountains. The snow had lost all its lustre. The constant shelling, and fallen soldiers from both sides, had turned the ground into dark shades of red and black. Captain Vikram Batra and Captain Naveen Nagappa were sitting inside a recently captured enemy bunker. The bonhomie in the middle of the war hadn't been forgotten. They were sharing a good laugh. Captain Batra, who was a year senior to Captain Nagappa, asked him, '*Oye, anna, tera retirement plan kya hai?* [Hey Brother, what are your retirement plans?]'

Captain Batra affectionately called Captain Nagappa 'anna'—i.e., brother.

He replied rather sadly, '*Pata nahi*, Sir. I am from the EME. I will leave the 13 JAK RIF [Jammu and Kashmir Rifles] in six months. I am only worried about whether I will meet you again.'

'*Anna, tu* JAK RIF *ke liye kyon nahi* opt *kar leta hai?* [Why don't you opt for the JAK RIF?] See, I have a very simple plan. If you join the JAK RIF, we will be together. Once I retire from the Army, I will open a strawberry farm at my place in Palampur. You can join me there. I will also keep horses, and we will have good fun.'

It was the usual crazy conversation for most souls at a far-off battlefield. Who talks of retirement plans in the middle of a war, where death looms round the corner every second? But this is how the valiant soldiers are.

Vikram Batra offered him some shakarparas from his bag. At that moment they realized that Captain Nagappa's fingers were coated with blood. He must have got it while bandaging or evacuating an injured or dead soldier as they captured the last bunker during the day time, but he had not noticed it until now. Captain Vikram Batra took his hand and rubbed some ice on it. He said, '*Jo tere hath me laga hai wo apne bando ka khoon hai. Jab tak tere hath mei dushman ka khoon na lage, chorna mat salo ko.*[This is the blood of our own men. Don't let the enemy get away with it. You achieve glory when you hands are stained with the enemy's blood.]'

That was the last conversation they had. Captain Naveen Nagappa picked up his AK-47, and rushed towards the last but one bunker to unleash his wrath and capture the peak at Point 4875. The last few days flashed before his eyes.

* * *

4 July 1999
The Base of Point 4875
Mushkoh Valley

In May 1999 the Indian Army found that the Pakistani military and some terrorists had crossed the LoC and infiltrated into the Indian terrority. They had occupied strategic high-altitude positions, which served as de facto borders. In retaliation the Indian Army launched a massive high-altitude mountain offensive, Operation Vijay, to evacuate them and recapture the peaks. The Operation finally concluded on 26 July 1999, after the Indian Army recaptured all its peaks successfully. Captain Vikram Batra and Captain Naveen Nagappa are names from the war that would be etched in the minds of the Indians forever. Captain Nagappa told me the details about how they prepared themselves at the last minute before launching the final assault.

Just a few days back, when Naveen returned from his reconnaissance mission at the captured Point 4875, he received some valuable information regarding enemy movement, weapons, change of guard, and other relevant things. Lieutenant Col Y.K. Joshi assigned Captain Vikram Batra and Captain Sanjeev Singh Jamwal to capture Point 5140.

Captain Nagappa was asked to create an ammunition dump at the base, and provide backup in case needed. Point 5140 was a huge victory, with no casualities. The morale of the troops was high, and the famous line from Captain Vikram Batra, 'Ye dil maange more,' won the hearts of millions.

Captain Nagappa remembers they could smell the victory in the air. Now it was time for him to prove his mettle. He, along with Charlie Company, led by Company Commander Gurpreet Singh, was tasked with capturing Point 4875. Captain Batra was asked to create an ammunition dump and act as a reserve at the base this time. He was down with fever at that time.

Captain Naggapa said to me, 'Before heading to the War, the soldiers were asked to write letters to their families, which remained unposted. The most difficult thing for me was to tell my men that the letters would be posted in case they did not come back. We also had to deposit our identity cards, so that our identities were not revealed if we were taken as Prisoners of War (PoWs). I remember every soldier opening his wallet and staring at the pictures of his family for a long time.'

The first assault on the first 'sangar' at the bottom of Point 4875 was a surprise attack at dawn. The Pakistani soldiers were carrying Universal Machine Guns (UMGs) and 30 mm mortars. After the attack, the Indian side captured some AK-47s, UMGs, pistols, mortars, and other ammunition while clearing the sangar. The first capture was a piece of cake, but they knew that capturing the rest wouldn't be easy as the sounds of the bullets had alerted the enemies in the next bunker.

The entry into the next bunker called the Area Flat Top was a narrow ledge. Movement was extremely difficult. Charlie Company under Captain Nagappa divided itself into sections, but still could not manage it. It was heavily guarded by the enemy. They showered bullets incessantly. There was a pause on the Indian side—a lack of action—due to the heavy fire. The company was stuck in its position. Nobody knew what to do. They could neither move nor retaliate.

Rifleman Sanjay Kumar Singh[29] volunteered to go scouting for the Company. He wrapped a field dressing (a kind of bandage used by the troops) around his palms and crawled out, lying low on that narrow ledge. He reached close to the enemy bunker up at an elevation, and pulled the hot barrels of the HMG with his hands.

That was the defining moment, which allowed the movement of his comrades. He then charged towards the enemy bunker, even though they were firing at him. His chest and the forearm were hit by bullets, but it did not deter him from his course of action. This was when his fellow soldiers got a boost and they were back in the game.

Eventually, Rifleman Sanjay Kumar killed three Pakisatni soldiers in a hand-to-hand combat. Then he crept towards the second enemy bunker with a fallen enemy's machine gun. The enemy soldiers, taken entirely by surprise, were killed as they tried to flee.

Captain Nagappa said to me, 'It was unnerving to climb the peaks with bunkers around. The Pakistanis would let us climb up, and then open fire. They were on full alert after the initial attacks. We climbed up, gaining inch by inch. We would dash, roll, fire, crawl, run towards a boulder and hide behind it, fire, and then choose the next boulder to cover ourselves. We applied the same tactics again and again. Somebody would give cover. The enemy would fire, and we would attack in return, while moving ahead on the narrow ridgeline. The movement became extremely difficult by 5 July. Our ammunition had also depleted. I called Lt Col Y. K. Joshi back at the base first thing in the morning and asked him to send the reserve.'

Inspired comrades, taking no notice of the treacherous terrain, charged at the enemy and wrested the Area Flat top of Point 4875 from them. By 5 July the 13 JAK RIF had recaptured the Area Flat Top completely.

Captain Nagappa could not even heave a sigh of relief before the Pakistanis launched an aggresive counter-attack. The young Captain displayed exemplary leadership qualities and courage. He retaliated fiercely, holding on to the peak. The first counter-attack was beaten back. As the situation had just reversed after the recapture of the Area Flat Top, now the Pakistanis were exposed while climbing up, while the Indian side had the advantage of height. The Area Flat Top was of utmost importance for the victory of Point 4875, and Captain Nagappa was not ready to lose an inch. After this attack, the enemy became more desperate and offensive.

* * *

6 July 1999
Early Morning

The troops were famished. They had had their last meal on the afternoon of 4 July. On 5 July there were attempts to send them khichadi, but it could not reach the C Coy led by Captain Nagappa due to the heavy shelling and carpet firing around. Captain Naveen Nagappa said to me, 'War makes you do unimaginable things. Survival is never predictable, and might throw the most extraordinary circumstances before you. Trust me, to survive in such circumstances you don't need intelligence or strength, but adaptability. We did just that. We dug out some ice. The upper layers were a combination of black and red due to heavy shelling and human blood, but we found the bottoms clean. We cut the bottoms and licked those to quench our hunger and thirst.'

Captain Batra from A Coy,[30] along with fifteen other men, joined C Coy. A wave of jubilation ran among the troops. Captain Vikram Batra had earned a great reputation after the successful capture of Point 5140. Captain Naveen Nagappa was also relieved to have his senior around. Captain Batra had always been his saviour.

Captain Nagappa also told me how he had once dislocated his shoulder back at the IMA, and was given rest for twenty-one days. His morale was down as it meant losing a whole term. So when he was discharged by the Military Hospital in the evening, he moved towards the Manekshaw Battalion Mess, feeling sad. As Captain Vikram Batra was the Junior Under Officer of his battalion, he was among the last to have his dinner. When Captain Batra found Captain Nagappa with stooped shoulders and a sad face, he stopped him and asked, '*Oye anna, kya hua?* [Brother, what happened?]'

Captain Nagappa told him about his injury. Captain Batra consoled him, and also shared his food with him. Captain Nagappa was not aware that Captain Batra also belonged to the 13 JAK RIF until the day he joined the unit. Captain Batra's presence filled him with new vigour and enthusiasm.

Only the last but one bunker was left for the complete capture of Point 4875. There was a boulder between the peak and their own bunker. The weapons were pointed towards the peak, and two jawans guarded that L-shaped bunker. Captain Batra and Captain Nagappa took their turns and returned once they had exhausted their AK-47s.

* * *

7 July
One Boulder Away from Point 4875

The irritated enemy threw a grenade at the bunker early in the morning. There is usually a time lag of three to four seconds before the grenade blasts. In the heat of the moment Captain Nagappa threw the grenade back at the enemy. Unfortunately, it hit the boulder between them, fell back at his feet, and exploded—damaging his legs severely.

The bunker collapsed. There was complete chaos. Captain Naggapa's ears were ringing, and his body was suddenly in total shock. Dust and rubble wiped out the visibility, and he started hallucinating. Even during those moments, when he realized that the enemy was running towards the bunker to recapture it, he picked up his AK-47 again and started firing back.

Captain Batra rushed towards him, firing his AK-47 all the while. He, too, knew this was a golden chance for the enemy to recapture the bunker. They somehow managed the counter-attack. The first thing Captain Nagappa heard was '*Anna, tu darna nahi, main aa gaya hu. Chodenge nahi.* [Brother, don't be scared. I'm here now. We won't spare anybody.]'

Then he dragged the injured Captain Nagappa out of the bunker, and ordered him to evacuate. There was no help at the exposed stretch within the enemy's firing range. The injured Captain Nagappa crawled all by himself till he found a boulder to take cover.

During his interview Captain Nagappa said, 'War makes you completely irrational. I was injured in the morning. My leg dangled. Fortunately, a soldier from my Coy spotted me and tried to evacuate me. He could have been shot. There was heavy shelling and the stretch was open. At one point I told him that if my leg fell off, I would carry it back so that the doctors could stitch it. I look back and think how impractical it would have been. Once, while moving towards the base on the steep gradient, the chap managed to put me on a stretcher and two other chaps carried me down.

'Even walking on those loose rocks amidst heavy shelling was an arduous task, leave alone carrying a man on a stretcher. God knows how many times they dropped me and picked me up. I was bleeding profusely and felt excruciating pain in my legs. When I reached the base battalion, Unit Doctor Col Rajesh Adhau gave me first aid immediately. He picked out the splinters from my damaged leg and put them on my hands. And all I wondered at that time was if it had been a mistake to come back. Maybe I should have stayed on and fought the enemy.

'On 8 July I was on the helicopter to 92 Base Hospital, Srinagar. All the helicopters those days were medium to short range because of the shelling, and did not fly high. My nursing assistant suddenly woke me up and said: '*Dekho Saab, Point 4875 pe Tiranaga lehara raha hai.* [Look, Saheb, the Tricolour's flying on Point 4875.]"

Then I got to know that we had registered victory on Point 4875. I was in extreme agony, and my body felt like a ball of fire, but there was immense happiness in my heart. Somehow I managed to sit back and salute the flying Tiranga from the helicopter. That was the happiest moment of my life. My nursing assistant said again, '*Saab is Tirange ki keemat chukayi hai humne.* [Saheb, we've paid a price for this flag.]'

* * *

15 July 1999
Research and Referral Military Hospital
New Delhi

Sharada had come to visit her son, Naveen, at the R&R Military Hospital. Her tears would not stop. No mother deserved to see her son in such a condition. Both his legs were severely damaged. The left leg had some calf muscle still intact from the blast, but the right leg had nothing much left. It was the excellence of the R&R doctors, who took chances at performing reconstructive surgery regardless. Captain Nagappa was in bad shape. His body was all curled up, and he was in great pain.

Sharada said, 'You should not have come back. You are in such a terrible state. You should have died there instead of going through all these things.'

Captain Nagappa had been in shock and trauma for the past few days, but nothing caused him more grief than the fact that his condition caused such tremendous sorrow to his parents. It still makes him feel guilty. Those were tough days. It took him around three years to be able to walk on both his feet without crutches, which was indeed a miracle. The doctors had declared that he would not be able to. He underwent numerous treatments and surgeries during those three years, but never for a moment did he lose hope. The warrior was determined to walk like a normal person and, eventually, he did.

* * *

September 2000
Tumkur
Karnataka

Two first-year students were reading an article in their college library about a Kargil hero not being able to get a job. Young Sowmya read the article aloud. It described how the Kargil heroes were being treated disrespectfully by their country. Despite the promises of land and employment from the government, the pride of Karnataka, Captain Naveen Nagappa, still visited the Vidhan Sabha on his crutches daily, but had not had any support from the state yet. The article also asked, 'Is this the way to treat our heroes, who have given everything for the nation?'

While they were in awe at the story of the young man, young Sowmya said to her friend, 'Shilpi, if the Kargil hero is not getting a job, we surely don't stand a chance. Let's bunk the classes.'

The young girls laughed hysterically. They didn't know that one day Sowmya was destined to marry the same man.

* * *

January 2002
Bangalore

Naveen had recently cleared the Union Public Service Commision (UPSC) exam, and joined service as an Assistant Executive Engineer, a civilian officer at the 515 Base Workshop, Bangalore. It had been a long journey of struggle and inspiration, of falling down and getting up all over again, with a resolve to never give up. Life had changed for him in many ways since the days at Point 4875, but he was thankful to God for the gift of life. Unlike him, 527 of his comrades had lost their lives during the Kargil War, including Captain Batra.

Naveen's mother insisted upon marriage, but he knew no girl would ever marry him. Nor did he intend to. Though he could walk without crutches, his right leg was three inches shorter than the left one. There was no great toe. He also suffered from partial paralysis apart from the deformity in his leg. The signs of the blast were a part of his identity now. He didn't ever regret that, but he never wanted a woman to enter that space. At times when he went out, but had to bear the stares and murmurs of people who noticed his limp or laughed at his crutches. They never knew his identity, and he didn't bother to enlighten them, but he was determined never to marry.

Captain Nagappa's aunt, who had recently met Sowmya at a marriage ceremony, insisted that her parents should give her the girl's photographs, which she later passed to Captain Nagappa's mother. The mother loved the photo, and urged her son to meet her family. Sowmya was still studying, and felt offended at the sudden prospect of marriage but, as time went by, and she learnt that the boy had fought at Kargil, she gradually grew fond of him.

Nonetheless, Naveen was adamant. He wanted to keep his pride intact, instead of facing a hundred questions regarding his legs, in the marriage market. Also, he did not want to push the girl into an association which would not be fair to her. It took the families six months since the talks were initiated, to convince Naveen to visit Tumkur, which was hardly two hours from Bangalore.

The first meeting did not go well. While Sowmya was dressed in her best clothes, the grumpy Naveen had pledged to present himself as shabbily as possible. For Sowmya it was love at first sight, but Naveen's grumpiness was beyond her comprehension. He did not interact much with her. Sowmya's family had their misgivings. The boy limped, and they had been told his legs were not completely normal either.

Later that night, when the boy's family had left, Sowmya's uncle and her mother immersed themselves in a family discussion. They concluded that the handicapped boy was not suitable for their girl. Sowmya was hurt. The humble daughter had never raised her voice in her house, but that day she could not stop herself. She said, 'I like the boy very much, and I have no problem marrying him.'

It stunned her family. Her father, Nanjundappa, was not convinced but, upon Sowmya's insistence, he said, 'I'd like to meet the boy once more, and see the condition of his legs.'

Sowmya did not like the idea. She knew that a man who had fought for the country, and saved its honour, would be a better match for her than anyone else any day. She knew she could only expect love, respect, and honour from him. She said, 'Appa, please visit him only if you intend to marry me off to him. If you don't intend to, please don't go. But I'd like to tell you—if there is any boy meant for me, it is him.'

Sowmya was aware of her father's misgivings at the prospect. Nanjundappa could not explain his insecurities about marrying off his daughter to a handicapped man, even if he was a hero who had fought valiantly for the nation. He had sincere regard for Naveen, but giving away his daughter to him was a different matter. He had promised her the best when he had held her in his arms for the first time. Pure love for his daughter blocked his mind.

Nanjundappa fixed another meeting with Naveen in Bangalore. Sowmya's uncle was also with him. When they met Naveen at his bachelor's accommodation, they requested him to show his legs to them. Naveen obliged them, but with hidden hurt and anger. This was precisely why he had never wanted to get married.

When the men returned home, Sowmya's mother, Shashi, asked them eagerly about the condition of Naveen's legs. Nanjundappa said, 'I don't know why the boy came here looking so scruffy. I met him at his house, and he looked so handsome. It was such a lovely meeting with him. He is so well behaved and gentlemanly. I hope he gets a girl better than Sowmya.'

Nobody slept that night. Sowmya could not take her mind off Naveen. Next morning she went straight up to her appa and said, 'Appa, I don't want him to marry someone better than me. I think I will suffice for this lifetime.'

Sowmya's younger sister, Kavya, too took great pains to convince their parents. She asked them: what if he had lost his legs after marriage? She said they should take great pride in what he had done for the nation. Eventually, they agreed to Sowmya's wishes. Sowmya was elated beyond words, utterly unaware of the trouble brewing in the boy's camp.

Naveen was hurt and unhappy about the whole parade, but one of his relatives calmed him down. He asked him to step into the shoes of the girl's father. The third phase of the marriage talks began. The boy's family visited the girl's family in Tumkur once again. But the vibes had changed this time. Naveen had taken great pains to dress himself up and looked every inch a gentleman, while Sowmya glowed in her green saree.

The incident that sealed their relationship forever was when Naveen asked Sowmya if she wanted to see his leg before making the final decision, and she said, 'No.'

The wedding date was fixed as 30 May 2004, and that was a rather beautiful start of the fascinating journey Naveen and Sowmya were about to take together.

* * *

March 2004
Bangalore

Sowmya was in the last semester of her college. She had to complete a project assignment with HAL, Bangalore. She shifted to a PG accommodation in Bangalore, not too far from Captain Nagappa's place. The courtship started between the warrior and his maiden, exactly the way they tell you in fairy tales. She would talk, and he would listen; she would smile, and he would be mesmerized by her smile. Seconds would turn into minutes, and minutes into hours but, no matter how much they spent together, it only felt like a moment.

Slowly, they discovered each other. Sowmya realized Naveen was nothing like that quintessential tough Army guy—all about guns and salutes. He was somewhat a calm, composed, caring, and affectionate person, who carried his heart on his sleeve. Naveen found his soulmate in the shy and sweet Sowmya. Little things brought a smile to their faces now and then. She had once mentioned to him casually how fond she was of teddy bears and chocolates. He did not forget to bring both a teddy bear soft toy, and a Dairy Milk chocolate, on their first date.

He loved it when she struggled hard to put an end to his extravagance and found pleasure in the simplest things. They both despised movies and would read books together, trying to find meanings in the stories—and they cherished their essence for a long time. Both detested crowds and noise, and the quietest of the places held a special place in their hearts. The connect between them was so perfect that they felt they had known each other for all eternity. Those were the best days Sowmya and Naveen both fondly remember.

Sowmya told me how she planned to return to Tumkur by the end of April, to prepare for the wedding she had eagerly waited for, but things don't always go as planned, right? She said to me, 'My sister and I were busy with the wedding shopping when I received my final examination dates. They were to begin on 1 June 2004, just a day after the wedding. It was like a bomb exploding in my family.

'My father had always been very conscientious with our education, and he tried to postpone the wedding date to July—after my exams had finished—but Naveen's mother was adamant. The date 7 July was considered inauspicious in their family since she herself had been widowed that day. It was also the date when the bomb had exploded at Naveen's feet and crippled him during the Kargil War.

'My father had always been a progressive man. He did not believe in superstition. He was truly concerned about my exams, and wondered if I'd be able to continue scoring a distinction. It was his greatest wish. Naveen would prod me to go ahead with the wedding. Eventually, I had to argue with my appa to convince him. I promised him I would study beforehand and obtain a distinction. But he was upset with me for a long time—at least until he saw a distinction in my results.'

She laughed a little as we talked, which filled my heart with warmth I cannot describe. Here was a woman who had got her Prince Charming but, even better, was privileged to have an amazing father for whom the daughter's education mattered more than her wedding.

* * *

30 May 2004
Tumkur

The Nanjudappa home glittered with fairy lights, and the smell of fresh marigold flowers emanated from every corner. The muhurtam had been decided for early morning. The rituals were taking long. Just a day before, on 29 May, they had hosted a huge party and the engagement ceremony in the evening—as is the custom in south Indian weddings. They were exhausted, but nothing could wipe the grin off Sowmya's face. She looked ethereal all clad in pink, while she stared at her Naveen slyly. And no one could measure the pride the dashing groom held in his heart for his new bride when he tied the mangalsutra around her neck. Today the happily married couple has a twelve-year-old daughter, Savera, who vouches for the love and affection her parents hold for each other. I could not stop smiling for days once their story was completed. I must have read it at least ten times by now, because finally I had found a story where the princess lived happily ever after with her knight in shining armour.

* * *

The story is based on the interviews of Mrs Sowmya Nagappa and Captain Naveen Nagappa, who are settled in Bangalore now. Captain Nagappa still works as a civilian officer with the Army. He was awarded the Sena Medal for gallantary for his exceptional devotion to duty, and exemplary display of courage at the time of adversity. For a long time Captain Nagappa could not gather the courage to revisit Point 4875. However, in July 2019, after twenty years of the Kargil War, he finally revisited Batra Top—which was named after Captain Vikram Batra when he attained veergati in the same Operation at Point 4875 on 7 July 1999 when Captain Nagappa was grieviously injured. Captain Nagappa completed the circle with other Kargil War veterans and Captain Vikram Batra's twin brother, where he had also lost other comrades-in-arms whose names are now engraved on the war memorial there. It was an extremely emotional moment for him. It took twenty years, but the city turned up at the airport to give a welcome suited to the stature of the hero, when he returned from Kargil the second time. Many said they came to welcome him because this was something they hadn't done during the Kargil War.

Acknowledgments

Now that the book has gone for a reprint so quickly, I feel fortunate enough to write the acknowledgment for a second time—an absolute dream for any author. It is also an opportunity for me to thank the people who supported the book tremendously after it was launched, making it a raging success. It is overwhelming to see that the book has acquired a cult status in the military world, where a Veer Nari is now being popularly called the Force behind the Forces.

Every story starts with an idea, and these extraordinary stories of our heroes and their wives started during the launch of my second book. The veer naris present at the venue expressed their desire to read real-life stories of Army wives. Many a time I decided to give up on these emotionally challenging stories of love and loss, but thanks to Vikas Manhas for reminding me about it being not just a book but also a cause.

Also, no words can describe the gratitude I have for the women mentioned in the book who trusted me with their most precious memories. There were love letters, pictures, souvenirs and gifts locked in trunks they opened again, for me, even though it brought them overwhelming pain. I am equally grateful to family members of the immortal soldiers—the mothers, sisters, fathers and brothers who were kind enough to share their heart with me.

Then there were brother officers, and fellow soldiers who stepped forward to share their bonds with the lost comrades. I am eternally grateful for that.

I would also like to extend my heartfelt thanks to the Additional Directorate General of Public Information, for facilitating the stories and approving the book for its authenticity and content. I also feel fortunate to have literary agents like Anish Chandy and Anushree, who ensured that these extraordinary stories found the best publisher. Working with ace editor Manasi Subramaniam from Penguin Random House also felt surreal. It's almost unbelievable how cordially we went through the process of editing and designing the book, even at moments of disagreement. Then there are Shubhi Surana, Aparna Abhijit and Divya who worked day and night on the stories we collectively believed in. A special mention to the cover design team as well as the designers. Everyone who has worked to turn this manuscript into a book shares a deep respect for our Forces. I might have written the stories, but this book is a personal tribute by each of us from the team behind *The Force Behind the Forces*.

Then, it brings me great pride to add a legendary name into my list of acknowledgments—Lieutenant General KJS Dhillon. The progressive and compassionate General extended a generous support to the book devoted to Veer Naris and opened many doors for me which allowed me to take my book to more Indians and connect them to the cause. I would also like to extend heartfelt gratitude to veteran journalists and news anchors from national media who helped me reach more Indians.

I would further like to thank my soldier managing the house along with his own hectic work schedule, when I was out for days, researching, travelling and interviewing people. He is the reason for everything beautiful in my life. I would also like to mention my parents, my children and my brothers who have always been my unshakable pillars of support and my zone of comfort. Their love for me is unmatchable.

And finally, I would like to thank my readers, and my social media family, for believing in my stories and making this book a grand success! This list of acknowledgments can now be closed with the mention of Mata Rani, the divine force in my life. It was she who wanted me to tell stories—that too, to inspire the world.

Notes

1. 'Laskar-e-Toiba terrorist killed in encounter in Pulwama', *Indian Express*, https://indianexpress.com/article/india/lashkar-e-toiba-terrorist-killed-in-encounter-in-pulwama-5572665/, 6 February 2019
2. 'Pulwama attack mastermind Kamran alias Rashid Ghazi killed in encounter', *Economic Times*, https://economictimes. indiatimes.com/news/defence/pulwama-attack-mastermind-kamran-alias-rasheed-ghazi-killed-in-encounter/ videoshow/68050555.cms, 18 February 2019
3. Major Vibhuti Shankar receiving the award, Gallantry Awards, Ministry of Defence, Government of India, https://www. gallantryawards.gov.in/awardee/4890, 15 August 2019
4. 'Pakistani army shells LoC for fourth consecutive day', *New Indian Express*, https://www.newindianexpress.com/ nation/2017/may/17/pakistan-army-shells-loc-for-fourth-consecutive-day-1605764.html, 17 May 2017
5. 'Major Kaustubh Rane's mortal remains flown to Mumbai residence', *Indian Express*, https://indianexpress.com/article/ cities/mumbai/major-kaustubh-ranes-mortal-remains-flown-to-mumbai-residence-5298392/, 9 August 2018

6. 'The tragic love story of Indian Army Major Shasidharan and Trupti Nair', ThePrint, https://theprint.in/features/the-tragic-love-story-of-indian-army-major-sashidharan-and-trupti-nair/178155, 15 January 2019

7. 'Meet Priya Semwal: The First Amry Jawan's Wife to Join As Officer After Her Husband Lost Life for Country', iforher.com, https://www.Iforh er.com/motivation/women-achievers/priya-semwal-first-army-jawan-wife-to-join-as-officer-after-husband-lost-life-for-country/, 5 December 2020

8. 'Sushma Swaraj calls Bahadur Ali "Living proof of terrorist who entered from Pak"', www.abpnews.in, https://www.youtube.com/watch?v=fwpDsofvWAY, 26 September 2016

9. 'Kashmir clashes over militant Burhan Wani leave 30 dead', BBC News, https://www.bbc.com/news/world-asia-india-36761527, 11 July 2016

10. 'Afzal Guru and the Jaish's jihad project', *Indian Express*, https://indianexpress.com/article/explained/afzal-guru-and-the-jaishs-jihad-project, 18 February 2017

11. SFA: Separate Family Accomodation is constructed for the families of soldiers serving in the field area, where their family cannot stay with them because of unsafe circumstances and uncertain climatic conditions.

12. '"Aaj Muqabla Hoga" Major Satish Dahiya's last words to Shabir Khan Before the Handwara Encounter', *Pune Mirror*, https://punemirror.indiatimes.com/news/india/aaj-muqabla-hoga-major-satish-dahiyas-last-words-to-shabir-khan-before-the-handwara-encounter/articleshow/57185762.cms, 16 February 2017

13. 'Major Satish Dahiya, braveheart to the core', *Tribune*, https://www.tribuneindia.com/news/archive/haryanatribune/major-satish-dahiya-braveheart-to-the-core-705487, 9 June 2021

14. 'PM Modi Pays Tribute To Soldiers Who Died Fighting Terrorists In Kashmir', www.ndtv.com, https://www.ndtv.

com/india-news/pm-modi-pays-tribute-to-soldiers-who-died-fighting-terrorists-in-kashmir-1659807, 15 February 2017

15. 'President Ram Nath Kovind presents Shaurya Chakra to Major Satish Dahiya of 13 Rashtriya Rifles', Doordarshan, https://www.youtube.com/watch?v=kaXbXBbp3Y8, 27 March 2018

16. 'Major Tahir Hussain Khan', Honourpoint, https://www.honourpoint.in/profile/major-tahir-hussain-khan/

17. 'Dhruv: Hindustan Aeronautics Limited', HAL, https://hal-india.co.in/Product_Details.aspx?Mkey=54&lKey=&CKey=24

18. 'Army Aviation Core', Indian Army, indianarmy.nic.in

19. 'Pathankot attack: all terrorists dead', *The Hindu*, https://www.thehindu.com/news/national/Pathankot-attack-All-terrorists-dead/article13982714.ece, 3 January 2016

20. 'Brave Daughters Salute Martyr Col MN Rai', India TV, https://www.youtube.com/watch?v=tQ6WiGYKTb8, 29 January 2015

21. 'Pilots Who Flew Crashed Dhruv Were Experienced. Chopper Has a History of Crash', ndtv.com, https://www.ndtv.com/india-news/pilots-who-flew-crashed-dhruv-were-experienced-chopper-has-a-history-of-crashes-739113, 12 February 2015

22. 'List of personnel being conferred gallantry awards on the occasion of Independence Day – 2016', Indian Army, https://indianarmy.nic.in/Site/FormTemplete/frmTempSimple.aspx?MnId=BQHP5qm8I2OY+qfysLPazA==&ParentID=Q98Kq/f6RXzCQhxRppMU5w==&flag=62lZRXDF39TnHN+AOSUAVA==

23. 'Four branded witches, lynched in Jharkhand', *Times of India*, https://timesofindia.indiatimes.com/city/ranchi/four-branded-witches-lynched-in-jharkhand/articleshow/70322751.cms, 22 July 2019

24. 'Lance Naik Raj Kumar Mahto', Honourpoint, https://www.
    honourpoint.in/profile/lance-naik-raj-kumar-mahto-2/

25. 'About AWWA', https://awwa.org.in/Home/About

26. 'Remembering Kargil: What is Battle of Point 4875?
    All you need to know', https://www.youtube.com/
    watch?v=THh338U5LSU, 26 July 2019

27. 'How Wounded Sanjay Kumar Facilitated Capture of Area
    Flat Top in Kargil War', My India My Glory, https://www.
    myindiamyglory.com/2017/05/16/how-wounded-sanjay-
    kumar-facilitated-capture-of-area-flat-top-in-kargil-war/

28. A coy is a body of troops comprising approximately 132
    personnel of all ranks consisting of several platoons. Each
    platoon is capable of launching an attack on enemy post
    independently.